FRANK WORRALL is Britain's No. 1 sports biographer and writes exclusively for John Blake Publishing. He is the author of sixteen books on sport, including the bestselling *Roy Keane: Red Man Walking*, *Rooney*, *Celtic United*, *Lewis Hamilton: Triple World Champion* and *Rory McIlroy: The Biography*. Rock star Rod Stewart once hailed *Celtic United* as 'the last good book I read'. Frank's website frankworrall.com has details of all his books and he can be found @frankworrall on Twitter.

JAMIE VARDY

THE BOY FROM NOWHERE

FRANK WORRALL

JOHN BLAKE

Published by John Blake Publishing Ltd,
3 Bramber Court, 2 Bramber Road,
London W14 9PB, England

www.johnblakebooks.com

www.facebook.com/johnblakebooks [f]
twitter.com/jblakebooks [t]

This edition published in 2016

ISBN: 978 1 78606 117 1

British Library Cataloguing-in-Publication Data:

A catalogue record for this book is available from the British Library.

Design by www.envydesign.co.uk

Printed in Great Britain by CPI Group (UK) Ltd

3 5 7 9 10 8 6 4

Papers used by John Blake Publishing are natural, recyclable products made from
wood grown in sustainable forests. The manufacturing processes conform to the
environmental regulations of the country of origin.

Every attempt has been made to contact the relevant copyright-holders,
but some were unobtainable. We would be grateful if the
appropriate people could contact us.

ACKNOWLEDGEMENTS

Special thanks to James Hodgkinson, Joanna Kennedy and all at John Blake Publishing.

Thanks also to Dave Morgan, Mark Fleming, Alan Feltham, Danny Bottono, Ray O'Shaughnessy, Tony Bethel, Dave Courtnadge, Ben Felsenburg, Alex Butler, Roy Stone, Steven Gordon, Pravina Patel, Colin Forshaw, Tom Henderson Smith, Graham Nicholson and Shaf Karim.

Not forgetting: Angela, Frankie, Jude, Nat, Barbara, Frank, Bob and Stephen, Gill, Lucy, Alex, Suzanne, Michael and William.

This book is dedicated to Dominic Turnbull,
a great journalist and friend,
and Drs Stephen Evans and Will Webb.

'He is aggressive, he is quick, he has got energy and he has got a goal in him. He has proved that. He has got assets suited to modern-day football. Vardy is a great example of never giving in and keeping a great belief in himself.'

Sir Alex Ferguson

'There was this very funny incident when we were training at Fylde Rugby Club. It happened to be the chef's birthday and a group of lads — Jamie included — decided to wrap this guy's whole car in cling film. There were bits and bobs on the car too — anything they could find! It was all taken in jest, very funny, and Jamie was part of a group of lads always involved in that sort of banter. If something had happened you could pick two or three who'd definitely be involved. Jamie was always a bubbly guy, always wanting to enjoy himself. He is one of the good guys.'

Danny Moore (Fleetwood kit man)

'From the day he stepped in the door I've been the biggest Jamie Vardy fan you can find. He epitomises everything I love about football — his aggression, his mentality and the way he works for the team. He's added goals to his game and for me, on current form, he's the best striker in the Premier League.'

Kasper Schmeichel (Leicester City goalkeeper)

'He's working class and he's our hero. He's a throwback to the footballers of old who used to climb up the ladder to make it in the top league. He's one of us. He's not like the other prima donna footballers. Vardy plays through the pain barrier for the club, even if he's got two broken bones in his wrist.'

CLIFF GINETTA (Chairman, Leicester City Supporters Club)

'I'm just a pest. That's all I've ever been. I don't know how to play any different. There is no sitting off, I just go straight at them.'

JAMIE VARDY

CONTENTS

CHAPTER ONE

IN THE DEEP MIDWINTER

The day is 11 January, 1987, and the Steel City is blanketed with snow. The locals shiver as they try to shovel up to eleven inches of the white stuff away from their front doors and driveways. Most don't bother, deciding to take the police's advice on the Radio Hallam breakfast show and stay at home for the day. It's an excuse to miss work – you can't get in if you're snowed up – and it's an excuse to miss a day in the classroom, since all the schools are shut for the day anyway. 'It's like being in bloody Russia!' one plucky old-timer jokes as he manages to make it to the corner shop to stock up on milk and bread. Some aren't so lucky and have to go without, as the city struggles through one of the worst winters in its history. The whiteout would claim eight lives and the Northern General Hospital would be overrun with accident victims.

Temperatures drop to minus 5.4 degrees Celsius – the lowest for more than one hundred years – and the big freeze shows no sign of easing. Into this unforgiving scene in Sheffield, South Yorkshire, on this particularly harsh winter's day, the footballer who would become the biggest name of the 2015–16 season is welcomed into the world.

To some, he would one day become a 'footballing messiah of the North'.

But to his happy mum and dad on that white winter's day, he was simply 'Our Jamie'.

Jamie Vardy was born James Richard Gill to dad Richard Gill, aged twenty-four, and mum Lisa Clewes, who was eighteen. Lisa would change her son's name when Richard walked out on them after getting another woman pregnant. Labourer Richard would later tell *The Mail on Sunday*, 'It is a real shame that things did not turn out differently. But his mother and I were really young and I completely lost touch with them after we broke up. Jamie was a cute baby – I used to feed him and change him and push him out in the pram – but her parents did not approve of me and I spent most of my time in the attic. He was still in nappies when I left. I saw Lisa a few times shopping with her mother but Mavis just walked off, telling Lisa to ignore me. I knew she had changed his surname.'

Jamie was brought up by Lisa and stepfather Philip Vardy, whom Lisa married and whose surname she and Jamie took. It was Philip he would call 'Dad' as he grew up in the shadows of Sheffield Wednesday's ground, Hillsborough. His upbringing would be steady and happy and Jamie was football-mad from the day he first kicked a ball. He would spend hours out in the street and the park playing the game with pals as they used jumpers for goalposts. He always wanted to be a footballer and at school told teachers that he would 'make it' and play for Sheffield Wednesday, the club he supported and loved.

It looked like that was more than just a youthful pipe dream as he signed to the club as a youngster and impressed those in charge during youth team matches. But at the age of fifteen he was left distraught when the club showed him the door, telling him he was 'too small' to make it as a professional.

'When I got released by Sheffield Wednesday, the club I'd supported all my life, it made me think football wasn't for me,' he would later say. 'As soon as that happened I never thought I would play football again. It was a real heartache as a kid. The reason I got released was I was too small. I wasn't physically built enough. It does hit you hard. I was very angry and upset.'

Indeed, he was so angry and upset that he turned his back on the game. He went to college but the football bug took a hold again when he was seventeen and a pal pleaded with him to start playing again. Jamie explained, 'He got me playing for his Sunday league side, Wickersley Youth, but you can imagine what that was like. The refs let you get away with murder. There were two-footed, knee-high tackles coming in at you and, to be honest, you'd rather not be going near the ball in games like that.'

Despite that, he started to make a name for himself in amateur football in Sheffield, and Stocksbridge Park Steels signed him in 2003. Steve Adams, then the club's youth team manager, told

Sky Sports, 'We played a cup game against Wickersley. They had a striker who was busy and fast, and I said to my assistant, "I wouldn't mind that lad in our team. It wasn't easy getting him [Jamie] to Stocksbridge, as he was showing his loyalty to his pal he was playing alongside at Wickersley.'

But Steve did persuade him to join the club. Dad Philip went with Jamie for a talk with Steve, and after twenty minutes he had agreed to sign. Jamie said, 'It was getting back to enjoying football and I kicked on from there.'

Yet he would spend four seasons in the reserves before finally getting his first-team chance. Club chairman Allen Bethel invited Gary Marrow, the first-team manager, to take a look at Vardy, and Marrow said he knew immediately that Jamie was good enough to play for the first eleven. Marrow knew that Jamie was a natural talent after watching him in training and in a five-a-side session, while Bethel had recommended him after being impressed with the young player's speed and energy.

Jamie earned just £30 a week in the first team at Stocksbridge, which wasn't enough to live on. So he also worked full-time as a technician at a factory that made medical splints. His job involved producing carbon-fibre splints that helped disabled people who had a condition called 'drop foot' to walk naturally. He described the work as 'rewarding' but admitted that it was difficult to fit in playing football around it. Often exhausted, he would put in a full week's effort at the factory and then play a game on a Tuesday or a Saturday for Stocksbridge.

He also had to deal with the fallout from an incident that led to his having to wear a police tag on his ankle for six months.

He had been convicted of assault, and the electronic tag meant that he had to leave night games half an hour before the end to avoid breaking a curfew. Jamie told reporters in 2015, 'I was out with a friend who wore a hearing aid and two other lads thought it would be funny to start mocking him and attacking him. I'm not proud of what I did but I will always stick up for a mate. So I defended him and it ended up getting me in a bit of trouble. I was playing in the Northern League at the time, for Stocksbridge Park Steels. If the away games were too far away, I could only play for the first hour or I would break my curfew. My mum and dad would wait outside in the car and it was often a case of hoping we were winning, taking me off after sixty minutes and jumping over the fence to get home before six o'clock. It was a hard time for me and my family. I had to be in the house from six at night to six in the morning.'

His performances at Stocksbridge were not going unnoticed – indeed, the scouts flocked to the Bracken Moor ground to watch Vardy notch goal after goal. They included visitors from league clubs and he had a week's trial with Crewe Alexandra. The local Sheffield daily newspaper, *The Star*, summed up his situation like this in January 2009: 'Jamie Vardy, star striker with UniBond League club Stocksbridge Park Steels, is on trial with Crewe Alexandra. The pacy 21-year-old, who plays wide or down the middle, is spending a week with the League One club, who began watching him last year. His performances have also attracted the attention of other clubs including Oldham, Cheltenham and Sheffield United. Vardy joined Stocksbridge's youth setup when he was 16 and has worked his way up through their Under 18s and the second team. He is top scorer with 16 goals this season.'

The trial at Gresty Road did not lead to a move; it was later revealed that Crewe boss Dario Grady decided he wanted a more experienced striker to beef up his team rather than a boy from non-league. But a move did materialise when FC Halifax Town came in for him. They had been the most persistent suitors and had most impressed him and his family. 'I think it was always going to be Halifax Town because they seemed to be friendlier, persistent and nice people, and they convinced him,' Allen Bethel told Sky Sports.

Bethel later also told reporters how the two big Sheffield teams had also come in for the player but not followed up their interest. Bethel said, 'Sheffield Wednesday came in for him, we offered them first choice as they were only six miles down the road and they said they weren't interested. Sheffield United came [to watch him] eight times. Neil Warnock said he'd sent one guy several times and said the club couldn't risk him because he has been sent off twice in eight games he'd been to watch.'

Steels' boss Gary Marrow said at the time how sad he was to see his star player move on but added that he wished him all the best and was sure he would do well at Halifax. He said, 'Jamie has been a pleasure to work with and goes with all our best wishes.'

Halifax signed him from the team in the eighth tier of English football in June 2010 for a fee of just £15,000. Six years later, when he was in the top flight of English football and playing for England, you would be lucky to get him for £25 million. In three years in the first team at Stocksbridge, he had scored sixty-six goals in 107 appearances. He had spent seven years at the club and was sad to leave Steels, who had helped him fall in love again with the game.

He was moving on to a club who were UniBond Premier League rivals, and that in itself was a surprise, as he was easily good enough to have starred for a Football League outfit. As *The Star* pointed out at the time, 'Whilst the much sought after Vardy's departure comes as no surprise, it is however perhaps surprising that a league club didn't take a chance on the talented player and their loss is undoubtedly Halifax's gain. Vardy hit 19 goals last term despite his campaign being blighted with injury and suspension having netted 22 the previous season when helping Steels to promotion via the play-offs. Steels said that 12 months ago an offer from Rotherham United was rejected by both the club and the player as they were only prepared to give him a three months contract.'

Yes, Rotherham were prepared to give Jamie Vardy only a three-month contract. But the Millers, as *The Star* pointed out even back in 2010, were far from the only league clubs to look a gift horse in the mouth back then.

Jamie made his Halifax debut on 21 August 2010, in the home game against Buxton, scoring the winning goal as Town triumphed 2–1. It was the first of many in that campaign as he grafted to help the club win promotion and quickly became their standout player. Now aged twenty-three, he hit twenty-seven goals in thirty-seven appearances in that first season – a feat that resulted in his being named the Players' Player of the Season. Towards the end of the campaign he almost notched a hat-trick of hat-tricks, failing to find a third goal only in Halifax's 3–1 win over Nantwich Town at the end of March 2011. The *Halifax Courier* reported his brilliant feat, saying, 'Jamie Vardy took his goal tally to an incredible eight in three games as Town's march towards the Evo Stik Premier Division title continued to gather pace. He struck in each half, with Liam Hogan heading home in between, as the Shaymen extended their winning run to five matches. The win increased Neil Aspin's side's lead at the top of the table to 14 points and kept alive their hopes of clinching a second successive promotion at the weekend.'

And Jamie had missed out on that hat-trick of hat-tricks by only a whisker as the Nantwich keeper saved his injury-time header with a fingertip. But his goalscoring antics were now becoming impossible to ignore and the scouts were a regular sight at the Shay. Would it be only a matter of time before he signed for a Football League club? It was the next inevitable step on his journey from nowhere to the higher echelons of English football.

A few days earlier, Town boss Aspin had revealed to reporters just what having Jamie at Halifax in his debut season had meant to the club, saying, 'When we signed him at the start of the season, he was a player not many people knew much about. Sometimes supporters look for a big name, someone who has played at a higher level. But I knew if we could get Jamie Vardy it would be a big signing for us. I had tried to sign him when

I was at Harrogate. He was always on the top of our shopping list and credit is due to the chairman, who backed me when I wanted to sign him. He's got better as the season has gone on, but certainly over the last few weeks his assists and goals have helped us out in many games. I'm just delighted he's at the club.'

Aspin also regaled reporters with the tale of how Jamie had turned up for his first training session in a rather less-than-professional manner: 'The first time I've seen him he was playing in a pre-season game for Stocksbridge against Sheffield United Under-21s and I only had to watch him the one time. You could tell immediately that he has great potential but when he first turned up for pre-season training, he didn't have the correct footwear. All the other players who didn't know who he was looked at him and said, "Who's that we've signed?" But, once he started playing, everyone realised we had someone who was going to be a bit special. I was convinced within one game. He played on the right wing; he played on the left wing all in the same game. He played different positions; there was his pace, his touch, so I didn't need to see much more.'

Clearly, he was a massive asset at Halifax – and Aspin, to his credit, had emphasised to Jamie upon signing that he would now play only at centre-forward rather out on the left or right wing – but his goals meant he would not be there long-term. They helped Halifax secure the Northern Premier League title for the 2010–11 season and many Town fans feared he might be snapped up then. Yet he was still at the club at the start of the next campaign for Halifax – but not for long. The player hit three goals in the opening four games of the 2011–12 season and his obvious goalscoring feats meant bigger clubs now began to circle like vultures.

Yet once again Jamie would defy expectations by remaining in non-league. It was as if his experience of rejection at Sheffield Wednesday all those years earlier had soured his Football League ambitions. But, according to sources who knew the boy, it was simply that Fleetwood showed him the love he needed to move. Never an insecure boy, he was, however, a player for whom the arm around the shoulder always worked better than so-called tough love. And he was ambitious and he did want to make it to the top of his trade; it was just that he seemed happy to take it a step at a time in the belief that he would get there in the end. Which, of course, he did.

So it was that, after those four games for Halifax in the new season, he moved across the Pennines over to Fleetwood on the northwest coast for a fee of £150,000. The club, based just outside Blackpool, had ambitions of their own to make the Football League and believed that Vardy's goals could help them win promotion into the bottom tier from the Conference National. Vardy signed towards the end of August 2011, and would wear the number 33 at Fleetwood. Always a popular character wherever he went, Jamie would soon become known as 'Vards' to his teammates. The team was strong already and Vardy only added to a potent combination of talents, with many pundits of the time agreeing that it was the best ever chance to win promotion from the Conference National.

The move meant he was now a full-time footballer, earning more than £300 a week, which was especially good news since he had quit his job as a full-time technician just days earlier. It was becoming too stressful both physically and emotionally to combine that work with a blossoming football career. 'We were constantly lifting the moulds into the oven,' Jamie would later recall. 'They were so heavy. Thirty an hour takes its toll. My back was just hanging off. I left and four days later I was full-time at Fleetwood.'

And Vardy would more than repay the faith shown in him by Fleetwood boss Micky Mellon and chairman Andy Pilley, who had combined to sell the club to him and persuade him to sign from Halifax. Fleetwood vice-chairman Phil Brown would tell reporters in 2015, 'Our chairman, Andy Pilley, came to me and said we should have a punt on Vardy and I am happy to fund the fee. I remember questioning his logic at the time, I have to say, though we laugh about it now, but I did think it was a lot of money at the time.

'We signed him on the Friday morning and he made his debut in the evening against York City. I do recall, he might be a bit embarrassed about it, but because he was playing that night and after everything had been concluded and all the paperwork had been done, I organised for him to go to a local hotel in Blackpool to relax for a few hours and get something to eat. I remember his dad going, "What, and we don't have to pay and we can have whatever we want to eat?" I said, "Yes, just help yourselves." I remember his dad replying along the lines of "Bloody hell, son, we've done all right here."'

That debut ended in a 0–0 draw, but within days he had grabbed his first goal for the club, scoring twice in a 3–2 victory at Kettering. The following week he repeated the feat with a brace in the 3–1 home win over Gateshead. Then, a week later, he continued his incredible two-goal sequence with a third brace, this time in a 3–1 triumph at Ebbsfleet United. It brought the scouts rushing from Football League clubs, many now questioning why they hadn't taken a punt on the boy. But Jamie is a loyal guy and he determined he would see out the season with the club who had shown faith in him. The goals continued to flow – with a fourteen-minute second-half hat-trick in October 2011, as Fleetwood strolled to a 4–1 win at Alfreton Town. Just four days after that hat-trick, he scored twice in the 4–1 home victory over Bath.

Propelled by Vardy's non-stop cabaret of goals, Fleetwood were marching onwards and upwards to promotion. They now stood second in the table, two points behind league leaders Wrexham, and would prove unstoppable as they headed towards the Football League. His feats earned him the Conference Premier Player of the Month award for November, and the former Stocksbridge Park Steels and Halifax Town striker would score a total of thirty-four goals in just forty outings for the Cod Army that season.

It was an FA Cup match at the start of January that signalled he was heading fast towards the big time. Fleetwood lost 5–1 at home to Fylde coast rivals Blackpool, but Vardy impressed, scoring his team's consolation goal. Indeed, Pool boss Ian Holloway was so impressed by the player he filed a £750,000 bid a couple of days later. It was rejected immediately by Fleetwood, who would also receive further offers before the transfer window shut that month. Jamie could have been forgiven for feeling let down, that his big chance had come and gone. But he wasn't affected one iota. He continued to knuckle down and repay the faith in him Fleetwood had shown the previous year, much to the delight of chairman Andy Pilley, who told the *Daily Mirror*, 'We had £1m bids in January and he had only been with us three months. But I desperately didn't want him to go because if he went we would lose a huge chance of promotion to the Football League. We managed to persuade him to stay for three more months . . . I was delighted because he could have spat his dummy out and been a pain to us after we didn't let him go in the January but he rolled his sleeves up and got the goals to get us promoted.'

Not only did Jamie's goals win Fleetwood promotion to the Football League, they also helped them lift the title. And his reward was to finally play in the League, but it would not be in the bottom tier with the Cod Army. No, his exploits had earned him a £1 million move to Leicester City and a stab at Championship-level football, with the prospect of the Premier League now just an enticing one division away. Yes, the boy from nowhere was on his way to being somebody special after years of toil in non-league. He was about to prove Sheffield Wednesday, and all the other doubters along the way, wrong.

And how.

CHAPTER TWO

THE POWER
RANGER

May 18, 2012: the date that would go down in history as dramatically changing the fortunes of Leicester City – and one player in particular. On that day, Jamie Vardy took another step on his long walk from football's foothills to the very top of the British game: the English Premier League. The news that City had signed a non-league player up at the King Power Stadium did not have the sports wires buzzing with anticipation as it would have if, say, Foxes had signed a top-flight star for a massive fee. But the fee itself did cause a certain stir on the Fleet Street sports desks. Although officially 'undisclosed', it was unofficially confirmed by reliable sources that City had paid £1 million for the player. Yes, £1 million for a non-leaguer – the first time that kind of money had ever changed hands between the top leagues and the realms of the amateurs and semi-pros.

So there was something in the air – the pundits had to take notice precisely because of that fee.

Swift reconnaissance raids were made to fill in the background. Non-league writers suddenly found themselves in demand – as did those with official or non-official links to Sheffield Wednesday and the amateur scene within the 'Steel City'. The player was linked to the likes of Ian Wright, who had also made the big league rather late in the day – but could we ever hope that he might be as good as Wrighty? Plenty of people inside the game provided glowing reports and even suggested that Vardy could be a bargain at £1 million. And also that he was a natural-born goalscorer and that he would have few problems adapting to life in the Premier League. Some even suggested he was good enough for England; that he was fast enough and accurate enough to even threaten the likes of Rooney for a starting spot. But that, most pundits replied, was taking the fairy tale a little too far.

Sure, the boy might score some goals in the Prem, but was he really good enough to be able to progress and make the England squad? Surely, people assumed, he was too old – if he was that good he would have been picked up much earlier in his career. No, the consensus was that Vardy *might* have a future in the Prem, but his most likely success story would be in the Championship – as a goalscorer of some repute in the second-tier at Leicester. To be a Premier League hero, he would first have to play there – and Leicester were hardly promotion favourites when he joined the club. So, no, it was considered too far-fetched to expect the fairy tale to end with

Vardy taking the league by storm – let alone doing the same for England and international football.

Of course, a fairy tale it surely was that a non-league player had made it into the Championship and at a record fee, but only a dreamer would anticipate the story taking further twists and turns. Vardy would serve Leicester well in the second tier and maybe notch a few goals if they ever were to get back into the big time, but that was his and their level, given the constant dramas and ups and downs that had blighted the club over the last couple of decades.

So, when Jamie did sign on that bright spring day in 2012, there was no massive fanfare and no rejoicing among City fans. It was commendable that their club were giving a lad from non-league a chance, but it was hardly time to get the bunting and flags out. It was not as if the club were signing Ronaldo or even Rooney, was it?

If only we had all known . . .

The signing would change the fortunes of not only Leicester City, but also of Jamie Vardy and the club's loyal fans. And force us in the press – and managers, scouts and football club executives – to radically rethink the value of signing players from non-league. For not only did Vardy's fairy-tale rise change his own life, it had a ripple effect on others in non-league who had thought that they would never get a chance in the big time. Vardy himself would help bring through more recruits, and clubs suddenly felt excited that they could also give amateur and semi-pros a go. There was nothing to lose apart from scouting fees and transfer fees – and that would also have a domino effect, bringing much-needed cash into non-league and benefiting the game within that arena.

Jamie Vardy's fairy-tale rise was seismic – for himself, for other non-league players and for the game at the lower levels. Plus it brought a fillip to Leicester and England . . . Not bad for a million-pound gamble!

Sky Sports broke the news of the deal, saying, 'Sky Sports understands Leicester City have agreed a deal worth £1 million for Fleetwood Town striker Jamie Vardy. Vardy is understood to have turned down offers from fellow Championship sides Cardiff City and Peterborough United to join Leicester.

'Sky Sports has learnt the striker is now at the Walkers Stadium, undergoing a medical ahead of signing for the Foxes. The Conference champions have agreed what is a record deal for a non-league player, and it could rise to £1.7 million. Vardy, 25, only joined Fleetwood last season from Halifax Town. Before that he played over 100 games for Stocksbridge Park Steels.'

Soon, others latched on to the news. The BBC revealed that Vardy had signed a three-year contract. And Foxes boss Nigel Pearson admitted he was 'delighted' to have finally secured the signature of the player he had been chasing for months. Indeed, he said he had tried to sign Vardy in the preceding January transfer window.

Jamie himself was 'over the moon' with the move. He told reporters, 'I got to sit down for a chat with Nigel and this is where I wanted to come. You see the facilities and I thought, "Yes, I can see myself playing here." And obviously because the manager wanted me as well it made the decision easier. He said he'd been watching me for quite a while. Obviously, if I've caught his eye I must have been doing something right.'

Vardy conceded it was a big step up the football ladder but was confident he was good enough to survive and then thrive. He said, 'The standard of the players is going to be a lot better. But I've played in the FA Cup a few times this year and managed to do well against the league clubs and hopefully I can carry that on.

'Competition for places can only benefit you. If you know you've got that much competition then you're just going to have to work that extra bit harder so you can catch the gaffer's eye. If you're not playing with any confidence, then you're not going to play well at all. You've always got to have that inner confidence and that comes with the goals.'

In contrast to the delight at the King Power Stadium, Fleetwood chairman Andy Pilley admitted he felt a loss because his star man was leaving – although he understood why he was off and wished him good luck in his new adventure. He even understood why Town fans might feel they had lost the best player to *ever* pull on a Fleetwood shirt. Pilley told Radio Lancashire, 'We always knew that Jamie was going to move on this pre-season. We wish him well because he's been fantastic for the club. We've fought for good terms and we're pleased with the compensation that we've got.

'He's been absolutely amazing and a lot of supporters will say he's the best player ever that has ever played for Fleetwood.'

Fleetwood volunteer worker John Hughes was also

convinced that Vardy is the best player ever at the club. He told the *Daily Mail* he admired the way Jamie had worked his way up after a tough start in life in Sheffield. Hughes said, 'Jamie came from a rough area of Yorkshire but you never had any problems with him, he was a lovely lad. Everybody here who's seen him play will look for his results at Leicester on a Saturday. He's the best player I've ever seen at Fleetwood. He has done well in not getting ahead of himself. He wasn't given an education through a big academy. He'd come into the bar after a game and all the kids would rush for his autograph. He wouldn't say, "Oh, sod off", he'd sign it and was just one of the lads.'

Town manager Micky Mellon was sad to see Jamie go but also understood why he was seeking pastures new and wanted to test himself at a higher level. He had persuaded Vardy to stay the previous January when Football League clubs started to circle and had been vociferous to the press when it was suggested the player might leave then. 'Jamie Vardy is a Fleetwood player and will remain that way until the summer,' Mellon said. 'There is absolutely no doubt about that. He was brought here to do a job for the football club and he'll finish that job off. For the minute he's fully focused on getting Fleetwood Town out of this division.'

Of course, there was an inherent admission that Vardy *would* leave in the summer – that the player had been assured the club would not stand in the way of his personal advancement. But he would first stay and battle during the following five months to help Fleetwood themselves advance. It was a fair trade: get the club moving up and they would get him moving up – and away.

Vardy kept his end of the deal by scoring the goals that took Fleetwood into the Football League for the first time. And Mellon would never forget the boy he had taken a chance on when he signed him from Halifax in 2011. He was so impressed with Vardy's talent that he insisted on a clause when the deal with Leicester was finalised that would see Town receiving up to £700,000 more if he did play for England. Mellon told the *Daily Record* late in 2015, 'When I was at Fleetwood we bought Jamie from Halifax. Right away, I could tell he was a lad way above our level. He scored 34 goals in 40 games during his first season. We had scouted him and knew there was something special about him. He had everything. More than anything, Jamie had the right mentality.

'When he eventually moved on to Leicester, we asked for a clause to be put in the contract. We believed he was so good that – if and when he played for England – we wanted [to get] paid.'

Mellon, by now manager of League One Shrewsbury, said Vardy was a player who was 'lightning fast, with ability, desire and passion' and that Fleetwood played their part in his development by getting him fitter and helping him tactically. And he humbly admitted he was immensely proud to have been part of the Vardy fairy tale, saying, 'He was also part of my rise up through the English leagues as well. So it has been a good deal for both of us. I'm grateful for that and I'm sure Jamie is as well. I'm happy for him and I hope he continues to do what he's doing. I just wish he still played for me now!'

And Fleetwood chairman Pilley also came over as nostalgic when he told the *Mirror* how he was proud to have worked with Vardy and to have been part of his fairy tale. Pilley said, 'Nothing fazes him at all, it doesn't matter whether he is playing in non-league with a hundred people or playing at Wembley. It matters not to Jamie and I would back him all day long – he is as cool as a cucumber. There is a common theme with Jamie because wherever he plays the team wins leagues.'

It is striking how all the way through Jamie's career – from Stocksbridge to Halifax to Fleetwood to Leicester – you never hear a bad word about him from the clubs or fans he has represented. He is genuinely liked and admired for the graft he has put in to reach the top and for the way he remains so very unassuming and down to earth, despite the trappings of fame and fortune. This is a footballer who remembers exactly where he came from and how hard life was – and never takes for granted his luck and talent. This is not a footballer who has no time for the fans – he will always make the effort to sign autographs and say hello when supporters seek him out. Whenever you see a photo of Jamie with a fan, he is signing a book, a paper or a shirt.

He is no 'Big-time Charlie'; Vardy remains a diamond moulded from a rough-and-ready background. You take him as you find him – and those at Fleetwood were sad to see him leave in 2011, as were the fans, the manager and the chairman. Meanwhile, Leicester – and boss Nigel Pearson in particular – were delighted to have won his signature.

Pearson, himself a man with no airs and graces, is a person

who can sometimes appear abrasive and too forthright, but of whom those who know him will not entertain any such criticisms. He was the ideal manager for Vardy when the boy left non-league for the Football League. The duo would get on well and Vardy liked Pearson for his straight talking and no-nonsense approach. Like Vardy, he did not suffer fools gladly, but, also like Jamie, he had a soft centre for those who got close. They would make an ideal pairing as they combined to take City back where they belonged: in the Premier League.

Yet, initially, footie fans of teams in the Football League remained unsure and sometimes unconvinced that the Foxes had made a good move in signing a non-league player. They wondered whether City wouldn't have been better off bringing in someone who guaranteed goals because they had already done the business in the Football League – someone like, say, Jordan Rhodes, at the time a prolific goalscorer at Huddersfield Town, who went on to prove himself just as goal-prolific when he moved to Blackburn (although he wouldn't cost £1 million, as Jamie did, when he moved in August 2012, it would take £8 million before Huddersfield finally relented and let him go).

On the fans' forums, a Crystal Palace supporter cautioned, 'I think Leicester City may be the wrong side for him. If the likes of Jermaine Beckford have bottled the expectation at Leicester City this season, there is an argument that a Conference-proven player will do exactly the same. A side like Bristol City, Millwall or ourselves – who would potentially allow a season or two to settle before expecting a play-off push under the current regime – would be better for his development.'

And a Sheffield Wednesday supporter argued that he was too old and not disciplined enough to make it, saying, 'A reserve team player at that age does not warrant a £1m plus transfer fee. At that age a player with no real first-team experience would be considered to have wasted their talent. If you speak to league managers that had him on trial, lazy and unfit seems to be a common verdict.'

But one Foxes fan urged them to give Vardy a chance, arguing, 'I'm willing to give him a chance to prove himself with the massive step-up from non-league to Championship. I hope other City fans do! They're not exactly known to give players time and faith!'

And another fan felt he had real potential – that he was fast enough and skilful enough to make the grade in the professional game, suggesting, 'He appears to actually be more a creative forward even though he scores for fun, seems a better dribbler than finisher, so much energy it's untrue.'

The fans may have been divided about the move – although Leicester supporters, to give them their due, appeared willing to give the player a chance to prove himself – but the consensus among the clubs chasing Vardy's signature was as one: that here was a forward who could create havoc with Football League defences – and maybe do so even higher up the scale. Sure, some had doubts about his temperament and whether he would be willing to knuckle down and learn and develop more. But the general belief was that Vardy would take his chance and prove himself a predator; that he would eventually prove to be a bargain at £1 million. That much was clear from the roster of clubs bidding for Jamie's services in May 2012. If Leicester had decided not to take him, there would have been no shortage of others willing to step into the breach and offer him a chance at Football League level.

Cardiff City, for example, who were pipped to the post for Vardy's signature when he left Fleetwood, years later still feel peeved that they missed out on the player. Cardiff boss Malky Mackay's £1 million bid for Vardy was also accepted by Town, but the deal foundered because financial uncertainty over rebranding the club meant focus was lost on transfer business. The rest is history: Jamie joined Leicester and Cardiff were left to regret the gem who got away. I have no doubt the fans of the Welsh club would have taken to him and adored him and he would have bonded well with them.

Vardy's legacy would live on at Fleetwood long after he had moved to the King Power Stadium. In May 2015, as Vardy was making his mark with England, Town announced they planned to build their future around the Vardy prototype. The plan was that they would no longer splash out inflated fees for players. Instead, they would try to create their very own Vardys from academy level – with the idea of producing a superstar like Jamie from youth development within five years.

Manager Graham Alexander outlined the vision to the press, admitting that Vardy had been the inspiration for the project. Alexander told the *Blackpool Gazette*, 'We want to be a club that will encourage good young players to join us and make a career for themselves. There's only really Jamie Vardy who has done that in the history of the club. He did a fantastic job for Fleetwood in a very short time.

'He wasn't a player the club produced but it was a stepping stone for him to go on to the Premier League. If we can produce a player like that ourselves over the next five years that would be a fantastic achievement. That's where success can be gauged, not on the pitch but off it too. The chairman is excited about that, about doing something a little bit different that makes Fleetwood unique.'

This was the outcome of that sale and purchase by Leicester from Fleetwood in May 2012. Jamie Vardy's £1 million move from non-league to the Championship had wide ramifications for many within the game. Now he had to knuckle down and show that he was the real deal: that he was worth the hype. And if he did so he would be laying a marker down for others – Vardy would be the pioneer for more non-leaguers to make the big time. A lot of pressure certainly rested on the boy's shoulders as he arrived at Leicester for pre-season training in the summer of 2012. And he would not shirk it.

No, he would embrace it.

CHAPTER THREE

BLUE IS
THE COLOUR

After arriving in the summer of 2012, Jamie worked hard in pre-season training and was hoping that graft would pay off when Leicester boss Nigel Pearson named his team for the first match of the season. He knew he had no divine right to expect a guaranteed place in the team and that there were other good strikers at the club. But he was a positive guy and believed in his own ability. He also knew that Pearson believed in him – otherwise he would hardly have splashed out £1 million for his services. The gaffer had seen much promise in the footballer, having watched him many times playing for Fleetwood, and believed he would be able to live up to that promise and make the step up from non-league to the Championship – and hopefully beyond. Pearson had been impressed with the boy's attitude and desire and recognised that Vardy would never be happy until he had achieved his full potential. He was a latecomer to the professional leagues but Pearson saw that he wanted to make up for lost time; Pearson had the feeling that in time Vardy would even prove a bargain for that £1 million fee – and he was right about that, too.

Jamie would be rewarded for his efforts immediately, as Pearson chose him for Leicester's first game of the 2012–13 season. He would start the Capital One Cup match away at Torquay on 14 August 2012. The first-round clash would see him start upfront with Jermaine Beckford, who had cost a reported £3 million from Bolton the previous summer. Pearson's faith in Vardy was also reflected in the fact that he had handed him the famed 'number 9 shirt' on his arrival at the club – and he would walk out proudly at Plainmoor with that number displayed on his chest. Jamie headed the fourth goal in the 4–0 rout, and Pearson admitted afterwards he was pleased with the debutant's showing and the attacking options that were now at his disposal.

Pearson told BBC Radio Leicester, 'It was a very good performance. They are always difficult games to negotiate because you are expected to win but that is easier said than done. It was a thoroughly professional performance. We had a host of chances. It was good to keep a clean sheet and we had good discipline at the back. With a very important game on Saturday it was good to get this out of the way in ninety minutes. You have to get all aspects of your game right and we played pretty well throughout and always looked a threat. We have an awful lot of attacking options this year.'

It was a fair assessment of the game and of the way his squad was now looking stronger. There are no easy games in the Cup, and you can only beat what is put in front of you – to win 4–0 away is always a good achievement. By the same token, Vardy could not do much more than score on his debut, even if it was in the first round of the Capital One Cup against a League Two team. And it was Vardy who made all the headlines, despite being just one of four scorers, along with fellow debutant Matty James, Ben Marshall and Lloyd Dyer. The Sky Sports website ran with the headline: 'Vardy off the mark in Foxes romp'. And the Football League's own website also focused on Vardy with the following passage: 'Jamie Vardy netted his first goal for Leicester as Nigel Pearson's Foxes cruised to a 4–0 victory at League Two outfit Torquay United. Vardy, whose goals fired Fleetwood into the Football League last season, began to pay back his £1 million transfer fee with his first goal for Leicester. Vardy wrapped up a comfortable victory in the 77th minute, heading home a majestic diagonal cross by the impressive Ben Marshall as Leicester cruised into the second round of the Capital One Cup . . . [and] only an offside flag stopped Vardy scoring his second.'

And Torquay's own website was also generous in its praise for Vardy and his teammates, saying, 'United were unceremoniously dumped out of the Capital One Cup by an excellent Leicester City side at Plainmoor. The Foxes put on a masterclass to saunter through 4–0 . . . a clever goal from Lloyd Dyer and Ben Marshall's blockbuster had Leicester cruising at the break and the visitors added two more worryingly easy efforts from Matty

James and Jamie Vardy in the second period. Leicester's strength was perhaps best highlighted by the quality sitting in the opposing dug-out, as the likes of former England international David Nugent, Scottish international Paul Gallagher and the excellent midfield pair of Andy King and Neil Danns were named as replacements by manager Nigel Pearson. Vardy made it four, glancing into an empty net from a long ball by Marshall.'

It was a telling point – Vardy had started at the expense of former England striker David Nugent, who had made a big contribution at the King Power. The website also highlighted that, out of a total attendance of 3,367, supporters numbering 1,166 had made the long journey from Leicester on the night, a fine reflection of the loyal support Vardy would begin to enjoy in his time at the club.

Those who travelled – and those who saw the match at home – were impressed by Jamie's opening salvo. One fan, AK, said, 'Good to see Vardy get off the mark. Will do him the world of good, his first in league football!' And another, Ric, commented, 'Encouraging start! Hopefully we'll be confident for Saturday now [in the Championship] and we can hit the ground running. Vardy getting off the mark is massive too, a strong start from him and he can be as good as he wants to be.' It showed that, like City boss Pearson, the fans were convinced Jamie would be a success and that the sky was the limit for him. He could 'be as good as he wants to be' and his first goal for the club, on his debut, showed that he very much wanted to be the best. He had not come to Leicester to tread water – he was here to make up for lost time; he was very much a man in a hurry.

The more goals, the better – and the quicker they arrived the better, too.

Jamie kept his place in the team for the opening match of the Championship season, the home game against Peterborough. He didn't hit the back of the net but made his presence felt in the 2–0 win. Goals from Wes Morgan and Andy King got the campaign off to a promising start for Vardy and the Foxes. Boss Pearson was happy with the contribution made by Vardy, especially as he set up the goal for King. Pearson was also pleased with the new boy's running with the ball, the fact he could speed away from anyone and his constant harassing of the Posh defence, which made for a most uncomfortable afternoon for the visitors. Pearson said there was an expectation that this would be a good season for the club and that many were predicting promotion after the investment in players like Jamie. He said he believed the newcomers and the team could live up to those expectations and that he was certainly not about to play down the possibility of a glory-tinged season, and told reporters, 'It was an excellent start. They gave us a tougher game than many expected. We stayed patient, pressed higher up in the second half and got the two goals. Peterborough pass the ball exceptionally well and I'm sure their game plan was to keep it tight, keep possession and get us frustrated. It is good to get off to a winning start because we know the expectation on us is going to be there. We all want success here – the owners, players and the fans. The Championship is a difficult division to get promoted from and we'll have to work very hard.'

Vardy's run in the team continued as the Foxes crashed 2–1 at

Charlton in a match they might have expected to have won, or at least earned one point. The defeat showed just how tough a league the Championship was and how difficult it would be to climb out of it into the Promised Land of the Premier League. Any one team could beat any other on any given day. It was a war of attrition and longevity; you might think you were on your way up but would be brought crashing down to earth the following week. There was no easy predicting of results in the Championship and you had to be mentally, as well as physically, tough if you were going to thrive. Fortunately, Jamie was all that and he was determined to keep his place in the line-up, even though it meant David Nugent remained on the sidelines. The former England man was none too pleased at being left out and made his feelings known.

But, like Vardy, he was a tough cookie and believed his chance would come again. It highlighted how difficult it was for Vardy to not only make his name at Leicester after his arrival, but simply to stay in the team when a striker of Nugent's obvious ability was battling against him for a starting spot. On the other hand, the competition meant Vardy had to raise his game and continue to produce the goods – for he knew there was real talent on the subs' bench waiting keenly to replace him.

It was that determination to stay in the team that spurred Jamie on and led to his first goal in the Championship for Leicester. Four days after the loss at Charlton, the Foxes went down again, this time in a 2–1 defeat at Blackburn. Vardy's only consolation was that he grabbed the goal that gave City some hope of saving the points. Vardy equalised almost on the hour mark after Nuno Gomes had put Rovers ahead. It was a typical Vardy goal, punishing a defender for a mistake when Scott Dann failed to deal with a long ball from Wes Morgan, leaving Jamie in the clear, and he had no hesitation in firing the ball home. Jamie then had another effort disallowed for offside, although he and his teammates felt he was onside and that the 'goal' should have stood.

As if that wasn't punishment enough, Vardy and his teammates could only look on in horror as Morten Gamst Pedersen hammered home an unlikely winner with ten minutes to go. Afterwards, Nigel Pearson and Vardy were clearly disappointed, since both felt that the Vardy effort ruled offside should have stood. If it had done so, the Foxes would have been leading 2–1 and the outcome of the game would have been very different. As Leicester boss Pearson said, 'Unfortunately the officials made some key decisions, which did not go our way. When Blackburn scored their first goal, a player obstructed Schmeichel and as for Vardy's effort, which was given offside, I'm not sure where that came from because he certainly was not. I grant you there was great skill involved in their second goal, but sometimes you have to endure games like this.'

Losing two of their opening three games in the Championship campaign had not been part of the plan: if they were to get among the promotion-chasers Vardy and his teammates would need to get a good run going. Confidence was key and a consistent set of results would enhance the feel-good factor around the club. It wasn't as if Jamie was playing badly, nor were the team for that matter. It was just that they did not appear to be having the rub of the green, as exemplified by the 'goal that never was' for Jamie. The losing streak had covered two games and would now include two more losses with a win sandwiched in between.

The Foxes were beaten 4–2 at home to Burton in the Capital One Cup and 2–1 away at Wolves in the Championship, with just a 1–0 home win over Blackpool in the Championship to break up the gloom. Jamie would miss the Cup fixture but would be part of the team that finally embarked upon that much-needed run of good results after the loss at Wolves. An eight-game unbeaten run, including seven victories, was just the tonic Nigel Pearson had sought as his early-season promotion favourites finally raised their game.

The run began on 19 September 2012, as Leicester beat Burnley 2–1 at home, and continued until 23 October, when Brighton were vanquished 1–0. In that sequence Vardy grabbed two goals and was playing well, fitting into the team and proving he could hold his own at this level. The win over Burnley was crucial in lifting the pressure on Pearson, whose position was becoming under increasing scrutiny. My friends at *The Sun* outlined just how vital victory had been, saying, 'David Nugent and Jamie Vardy marked Leicester's second-half comeback with the goals that will ease the pressure on under-fire manager Nigel Pearson. Local websites have been filled with calls for his dismissal but last night's fightback silenced the boo-boys.

'His assistant Craig Shakespeare admitted: "We're pleased. We knew we needed to win this one."'

Nugent had put the Foxes ahead and Vardy won it ten

minutes into the second-half with a shot that bounced in off a Burnley defender. Even Burnley boss Eddie Howe had noted that Pearson was struggling to appease his supporters and keep a sense of optimism alive at the club. Howe said, 'We frustrated Leicester in the first half and the home supporters weren't happy. But conceding so soon in the second half was a killer, followed by a crucial deflection for the second goal.'

Nonetheless, it proved to be a sweet moment for Vardy; he had certainly repaid a chunk of the £1 million Pearson had invested in his services with his first goal at home for Leicester. That goal had lifted the pressure on the manager when he had looked in big trouble, and could be said to have helped save his job, given the catcalls and disillusionment among the fans. It also, of course, set up the confidence and lifted the mood within the camp that enabled the team to embark upon that unbeaten stretch of games. Vardy had also played a major role in helping co-striker Nugent make a personal piece of history. It was Jamie who set him up for the equaliser just after half-time – Nugent's hundredth league goal but his first of the season, after an eleven-match dry spell.

Nugent said, 'The gaffer mentioned I was stuck on ninety-nine in the team talk, so there was a bit of pressure on me to score. It wasn't the greatest, but, when you haven't found the net in eleven games, I'll take it. It's my longest streak without a goal.'

In some ways, it was surprising that the team were already facing such a fans' backlash, as the win meant their 100 per cent home record remained intact. But it was the form away from the King Power Stadium that had concerned supporters because they had lost all three league games. The fans were expecting more, given the investment in players during the close season, including that payment for Vardy's arrival. He was on the scoresheet again a fortnight later, as the team won 2–1 at Middlesbrough. This was a big win, as the Boro had also been unbeaten at home at the start of the season and many pundits had predicted that they would beat Leicester to maintain their 100 per cent start at the Riverside.

Vardy pounced on a deflected Nugent effort to equalise after Nick Bailey put Boro ahead and sub Lloyd Dyer claimed the points and their first away win for Leicester, which left a relieved Pearson delighted. He said, 'I think maybe we got lucky, but, given the way things have gone against us so far this season, maybe we deserved to get a bit of a lucky break. Tony Mowbray has pointed out that he thought the first one was offside and maybe he has a case and for the second one, yes, maybe there [were] some question marks over the free kick for the second. But, as I say, we have deserved to get the rub of the green, and, to be fair, we did create a lot of chances. We did help make our own luck.' The win pushed Leicester up to fifth in the Championship table.

But, after scoring at the Riverside, Vardy found the goals hard to come by and his season started to fall away as the pressure seemed to get to him. That goal at Boro came at the end of September and it would be 8 December before he found the net again. His goal came in the last minute of the home game against Barnsley and earned the Foxes a 2–2 draw. The last-gasp equaliser was a confidence booster to the player who had come on as a substitute for Martyn Waghorn in the sixty-eighth minute. Vardy was pleased to have ended his goal drought and to be able to show that he could still do a job for the club. He had earned the right to celebrate that night and hoped he had turned the corner. His boss Pearson was also glad that his £1 million man had delivered, and believed the Foxes should have won all three points, telling reporters, 'We started the game very well, scored an early goal but conceded two really poor goals and we gave a side that hadn't been in the game something to hang on to. They came here to frustrate us and it was hard to break them down. For 90 per cent of the second half we were camped in their half but they made the route to goal very blocked. They wasted time when they could, but ultimately when we were on top we gifted them two goals, and that's the biggest disappointment.'

The Star in Barnsley and Sheffield made the point that it was rather ironic that Jamie was the man to deny his fellow Tykes a win, reasoning that, 'A last-minute goal from South Yorkshireman Jamie Vardy gave Leicester a share of the spoils against Barnsley, but the promotion hopefuls will consider it two points dropped against struggling Barnsley. Former Stocksbridge Park Steels man and Sheffield Wednesday junior Vardy struck home from close range after good work from David Nugent, but Keith Hill's side deserved the plaudits after a battling show.'

But the goal would not prove to be a turning point for Jamie. He continued to struggle for top form and did not score again during the rest of the season as the club clawed their way into the Championship play-off finals. Leicester would ultimately fail to make it into the Premier League after they lost 3–2 on aggregate to Watford in the play-off semi-finals on Sunday, 12 May 2013. But Vardy's season ended two months earlier, when he played his final match of the campaign as Leicester drew 1–1 at Cardiff on Tuesday, 12 March. He came on as a substitute for David Nugent with nine minutes to go. It was a sad and disappointing end to his season, one that had started with so much promise after his £1 million move from Fleetwood, but that had fizzled out early, leaving him low and considering his future as a footballer. He had made a total of twenty-nine appearances for Leicester and scored just five goals.

It left him at the mercy of some irate fans on social media, and the man who had always had an inner belief and strong measure of self-confidence now started to doubt himself – and even whether he had a future in the professional game. A year later he would admit that the confidence in him of his then Leicester 'gaffer' Nigel Pearson and his assistant Craig Shakespeare was a defining factor in persuading him to push on and continue. Jamie told BBC TV's *Late Kick Off Midlands*, 'Yes I did nearly give up to be honest with you. But I had a few chats with the gaffer[s] and they constantly told me I was good enough and they believed in me and stuck by me. I'm glad to be showing the faith they showed in me on the pitch. I also know a lot of hard work has gone into it on my behalf as well as people believing in me. The gaffer has always said that he believes in me, even last year when I was at a bit of a low. It was a big learning curve . . . it was tough, I came into a dressing room with a lot of big names in and I wasn't used to it whatsoever. It did take a lot to get used to . . .'

The good news was that Vardy would take on board the encouragement and work extra hard in pre-season training. His confidence would return and so would the goals for which he was famed, and for which Pearson had splashed out that £1 million. If the 2012–13 season had been a character-building campaign that he had managed to survive, the next would be one in which Leicester fans would see the true potential of Jamie Vardy.

CHAPTER FOUR

JUST CHAMPION

If the second half of the 2012–13 season had been a massive anticlimax and period of depression for Jamie, the start of the new season in August 2013 would be the exact opposite.

He had been grateful to Nigel Pearson and Craig Shakespeare for their support and encouragement in May 2013, when he had seriously considered quitting the game, and now would be payback time. Jamie would hit the ground running in the Championship and looked to be a completely different player. That had been a result of the rest he had enjoyed since the end of March, with a relaxing summer holiday and time with his family, plus the hard graft he had put in during pre-season training. Vardy's self-belief and confidence in his own ability had clearly returned, and for Pearson it was as if he had signed a new player, such was the contrast in his performances.

The fans were delighted, too: here was the striker they had been promised and even the few who had booed him now praised him. The truth of the matter was that even the usually confident Vardy had suffered a bout of doubt and anxiety after the £1 million move from non-league to the Championship. But now the doubts had gone and the true Jamie Vardy would show the world just what he was capable of. He was, without a doubt, good enough to play in the Championship but his displays would also illustrate that he was talented enough for the Premier League – and maybe even the international arena.

It was a thrilling turnaround and a delight to witness for fans at the King Power Stadium, and beyond, as the boy from nowhere now showed he truly belonged in the big time. This term he would notch sixteen goals in forty-one games – more goals and more games as his performances justified his place in the Leicester first eleven. Pearson showed his belief and trust in the boy in the opening game of the new 2013–14 campaign, starting him up front at Middlesbrough on 8 August. The previous season it had looked at times as if he and former England striker David Nugent were competing for a starting role and Nugent would now once again revert to his place on the subs' bench.

The Foxes fell behind at the Riverside but second-half goals from Danny Drinkwater and Vardy won the game for the visitors. Ironically enough, it was Nugent who set up Vardy for the winner, with the latter making no mistake with his shot before reeling away in celebration. One game, one goal – it had been how Jamie had visualised his move to

Leicester would be when he arrived the previous season. He had started off well enough in that first season and then his form and confidence had fallen away. The key to success now would be to ensure there was no repeat of this, and he and Nigel Pearson were both extremely confident there would be no hiccup this time around.

Vardy told pals he was 'made up' with his goal and the win and that he now intended to build on it. And Pearson praised him for being a goal 'poacher' and for being so elusive when it came to beating defenders. The boss was also pleased with his team's overall display, for not only had Jamie suffered a crisis of confidence towards the end of the previous season, but the team and the club in general had been on a low after the play-off defeat to Watford had condemned them to another season in the Championship.

The initial aim of the new campaign was to blow away those cobwebs of despondency and aim higher, in the hope that they could win automatic promotion and avoid the heart-breaking lottery of the play-offs. Pearson said after the win at the Riverside he believed the result had gone some way to doing just that, and added, 'In the first half we didn't work hard enough, we didn't make enough positive decisions and we let Middlesbrough shape the game. But in the second half we made a few more positive decisions, worked harder and got our reward. We scored two very good goals, could have had a few more and possibly should have had a penalty. We were well worth the win, although it looked a bit precarious at half-time.'

One of the efforts he was talking about that could have

ended in another goal came three minutes from time, when Jamie latched on to a pass from Drinkwater, raced clear of the Boro defence and hit a low shot, which the keeper managed to push onto the post. No matter, Vardy was back in business, and so were the Foxes, and it was heartwarming to see him celebrate his goal in front of the fans who had travelled up from the Midlands.

Vardy then went two games without scoring but was back among the goals in the 3–2 home win over Birmingham at the King Power on 24 August. He had not lost confidence in those two barren matches and knew that, if he kept plugging away, the goals would come. No way was he mentally or emotionally returning to the crisis point that he had experienced the previous season. He was faster, he was dangerous and he was a menace, and, as he likes to say himself, a 'pest' to opposing defenders. The goal against Brum came after the Foxes fought back from 1–0 down. It was a relief for the club when Jamie struck on seventy-eight minutes to equalise Matt Green's twelfth-minute opener. Goals from Andy King and Nugent completed the win, even though City suffered a late scare when Chris Burke netted for Brum.

The stats boys pointed out that Leicester's ten points from four games, which left them with an unbeaten start, was only the second time in twenty-two seasons they had hit double figures so soon. It was also the first time since their 2008–9 promotion season they had achieved the feat. Back then, it was promotion from League One. Now, if the omens were anything to go by, could it be elevation to the Premier League at the end of the season? Vardy certainly hoped so, for it would complete his dream if he could make it to the top flight of English football – from non-league nobody to top-league striker in four remarkable years.

Pearson, as per usual, refused to even countenance such thoughts, especially so early in the season. He was a realist and a man who worked on hard results, not dreamy targets. His concern was the win just chalked up over Brum and the next match and three more points. Pearson was no automaton, far from it: he was one of the toughest managers to interview by virtue of his absolute insistence on straight talking and no nonsense. However, on this occasion, he indulged in a little banter with the gentlemen of the press – it was, after all, the week of his fiftieth birthday. Asked if he was happy that the team had moved up to second in the table after grafting for the win, and whether that was a good birthday gift, he replied, 'That is the key in this division – somehow grinding a win out of difficult situations. So you can certainly call me quite a happy fella!'

Vardy's run of fine form continued as City now crushed Carlisle 5–2 away in the Capital One Cup. He wasn't on the scoresheet but he was instrumental in sending the home defence into a spin with his runs and threat and he won the penalty that Chris Wood rammed home to make it 4–1 on the hour mark, also ensuring that Wood claimed the second goal of what would be a hat-trick against the League One strugglers. Leicester assistant manager Craig Shakespeare said, 'We're a good team when we pass and move. Carlisle won't come up against that very often in the league they're in.' The victory was so comprehensive that City could afford to replace Jamie on the hour for Martyn Waghorn, to keep him fresh for the more testing Championship examinations to follow. The view of the Leicester management was that you don't gamble with the player who was rapidly becoming your main man when there's no need.

And, just a couple of days after the win at Carlisle, the bosses told the *Leicester Mercury* just how much they were impressed with Vardy and how he had developed as a player and a man since the troubles of the previous March. Shakespeare told reporters, 'He is not just about contributing with the ball, he is contributing off the ball by pressuring defenders into mistakes. That is part of his game and if he continues like that you'll see what an asset he will be.'

City boss Pearson added, 'He's back to the player we signed in the sense that he's not turning down shooting opportunities and he's playing with confidence. If you talk to any striker, it's about confidence. It's a big step-up coming from Conference football to the Championship, but I've always had a lot of belief in Jamie. Last year was a steep learning curve for him and he's come back this season in good physical shape. But he also has probably got a bit more self-belief. He is the right sort of player for us.'

By October 2013 both Vardy and City were flying high. The team were living up to their tag of promotion contenders and Jamie was continuing to make life miserable for other sides. His input could be measured by two consecutive games that month in which he made the difference in very tight encounters. On

19 October, he scored in the 2–1 home win over Huddersfield and a week later also found the back of the net in the 2–1 home win over Bournemouth. As the scorelines suggest, in both games there was little to separate the teams. Vardy opened the scoring in the victory over the Terriers and an own goal made it 2–0, with another own goal making it 2–1. Pearson admitted he was 'delighted' with Jamie's performance and the win pushed them up to third in the Championship table, just a point off the automatic promotion spots.

Then, Vardy's winner against Bournemouth left them second in the table, and in those much-coveted spots. He made it 2–1 after taking the ball around the keeper and slotting it coolly home. It rounded off a sixth successive home win for the Foxes and kept them bang on target for promotion. It also highlighted Vardy's growing importance to the team, how his ability as a master poacher of goals could provide the difference between taking six points from two games and taking two points for what would have been two draws without his goals. Pearson was indebted to Vardy after that fourth goal of the campaign, against the Cherries, and the way Jamie kept his cool to round the keeper, Ryan Allsop. The boss told the press, 'It was an entertaining match, we were exciting going forward and we got two good goals. We deserved to win and put in a good performance against a very decent side.'

At the end of November 2013, Jamie bagged a brace in the 3–0 win over Millwall at the King Power. Now wearing an unlikely beard, he helped propel City three points clear at the top of the Championship. His first goal was one of the more remarkable ones of his career, starting way back in his own team's penalty box early in the second half, when City stopper Kasper Schmeichel rolled the ball out to him. Jamie darted the full length of the pitch, past his own players and the opposition, before firing home at the end of the run. He made it 2–0 minutes later with a more traditional Vardy goal, profiting from a defensive error, nipping in and shoving the ball past the hapless keeper.

Nigel Pearson paid tribute to the double effort, saying, 'I was very pleased for Jamie Vardy. I don't think anyone who watches us would have anything but praise for his tireless efforts on behalf of the team. He's grabbed his chance today and I know his teammates will be very pleased for him to get two goals. Last week it was David Nugent scoring two goals, and this week it is Jamie. We've earned the right to be where we are at the moment. But let me add, we are still only a third of the way through the season. Other results have worked in our favour, and that always helps. Even so, this was definitely a performance to please, even though the result is always the most important thing. I have a squad of eighteen players, or more, in whom I can be totally confident.'

Pearson remained ever the pragmatist even as his team seemed on an inexorable journey to the Premier League. Jamie was particularly pleased with the boss's praise – he and Pearson had both come a long way from the distresses of the previous season. Even the defeated Millwall gave credit where it was due, with their official website describing Vardy's goal feats in this way: 'Lloyd Dyer had already fired the home team ahead on 12 minutes, but it was Vardy's devastating quick-fire double that proved decisive to send The Lions spinning to another awayday loss and down to fourth from bottom in the division. Vardy grabbed his first – and Leicester's second – of the game seven minutes after the restart when play broke quickly from a Millwall corner and he skipped past Justin Hoyte to fire a low shot into the back of the net. The Foxes striker doubled his tally just three minutes later, taking advantage of defensive hesitancy on the edge of the area from Scott Malone to nip in and beat [keeper] Forde from an acute angle.'

Jamie's final goal of 2013 came in a crunch match at Loftus Road, just before Christmas. Again, his strike made the difference as City ran out 1–0 winners against fellow promotion battlers Queens Park Rangers. It was a good ending to a year that had been problematic in March and finally got back on track when the new season began in August. From at one stage considering quitting, Vardy was now the toast of Leicester as he continued his fine form, and was grabbing the goals that made a difference in tight contests. His goal just before half-time meant the end of QPR's unbeaten home record thus far that season, but also struck a psychological blow in City's favour. It toppled the hosts from the summit of the Championship in favour of Burnley and consolidated City's own climb onwards and upwards. They remained third in the table but were now there only because QPR had the better goal difference. Both were on forty-two points and Vardy's winner suggested it would be Leicester who would push on in the New Year. The loss was a blow for the hosts' confidence and they also suffered the indignity of Joey Barton being sent off.

City had suffered their own wobble, taking just one point from their three previous league games, but Vardy had put them back on track with his winner. And it was a typical Vardy goal – he left defender Richard Dunne for dead with his pace and coolly slammed the ball home past the hapless Rob Green. Jamie was proving he was the man for the big occasion and Pearson was grateful for that; whenever City needed a goal or some inspiration Vardy seemed to be the go-to man. After the match Pearson told the press that Vardy's goal had secured a vital win and put his men back on track for automatic promotion after that worrying three-game wobble. And he added, 'We did well today, we needed the win. I felt we created good opportunities, but I think they will probably feel they should have got something out of the game. We only scored one goal again, but the key is that we've kept a clean sheet and we've not kept enough of those this season.'

Vardy and City got better and better as the season progressed. January 2014 found them winning four of their five league games with Jamie scoring three times. In the 4–1 win at home over Derby, he scored the final goal and won a penalty as City stormed four points clear at the top of the table. It was extra sweet for the fans as Vardy put local rivals Derby to the sword in their heaviest defeat of the season. Vardy won the spot kick just after the hour mark, when he was scythed down by Craig Forsyth, with David Nugent making no mistake from the spot. A few minutes later Nugent repaid the compliment, setting

Jamie up for a simple shot to make it 4–1. More good news would follow: City were about to confirm the signing of the relatively unknown winger Riyad Mahrez. The twenty-two-year-old French Algerian would join from French Ligue 2 side Le Havre on a three-and-a-half-year contract for a fee reported to be £400,000.

Most fans scratched their heads when confronted with the transfer, but little did they know that Mahrez would, two years later, become known as 'the Algerian Giggs' as he terrorised defences in the Premier League and became the focus of transfer speculation involving the likes of Manchester United and Barcelona. Much as Vardy would be recognised as a £1 million bargain in 2015–16, so Mahrez would be seen as a snip – who could command a fee of upwards of £30 million if Leicester ever chose to sell. So January 2014 was indeed a momentous month for Vardy, Mahrez and the Foxes: they were all heading for the big time.

The 4–1 win over Derby was also the ideal birthday present for Jamie, who turned twenty-seven on the day after the game. He said, 'It was a good performance from everyone and you could have given anyone Man of the Match. We gelled brilliantly and got the result we all wanted. I'm happy to get a goal as well, so it is a little early birthday present. I won't be celebrating too much because I will prepare properly during the week for Leeds.'

He said that no one at the club was taking promotion for granted and that they were all keen to avoid the play-offs after the defeat at the hands of Watford the previous year, telling reporters, 'We have to keep our feet firmly on the ground. We know we have to keep picking points up. We will get on the training ground this week and work hard towards Leeds on Saturday. Confidence has been sky-high for a while. We don't want the same heartbreak we had last season, with how it happened. It's gelled the team together even more. Everyone just clicked in this game. We have to keep the performances going now and, hopefully, this will be our year.'

Jamie also netted in the 2–0 win over Middlesbrough and 2–1 triumph over Birmingham at the end of the month and added another couple of goals to his account in March as the Foxes marched on towards their promotion target. They beat Charlton 3–0 at the King Power on the opening day of the month – a win that put them seven points clear at the top of the table from second-placed Burnley and also meant they were thirteen points ahead of third-placed Derby, who led the play-off zone teams. It was a remarkable achievement considering the struggles of the previous season for the team and for Jamie. He had put them 1–0 up after ten minutes against Charlton with a typical poacher's strike in the box and the fact that the team had scored sixty-two goals so far – the highest in the Championship – was testament to the attacking football they played. Jamie was a part of a goalscoring machine and was enjoying his football immensely. Pearson, inevitably, tried to keep a lid on the euphoria, saying, 'We played very well and showed that, as the side leading the table, we deserve to be there. But we've got thirteen more games to go and thirty-nine points to play for.'

But Charlton boss Chris Powell painted more of a true scenario, saying he was simply happy the defeat was not heavier after the bombardment from Vardy and co., and adding, 'They're a very good side and we've possibly played against the champions elect if they carry on the way they're playing.'

Ten days later Vardy was at it again, this time netting a brace in the 3–0 triumph at Barnsley. It seemed nothing could stop the juggernaut: the Foxes were on their way to the Premier League with Vardy driving with skill and speed. Jamie fired home after twenty minutes and then even set up the second goal for Danny Drinkwater just before the hour mark. The master goal poacher found the net himself again four minutes later to settle the contest, latching on to a pass from Mahrez and, as he had done many times before in his career, rounding the keeper and slotting the ball home. The win put City eight points clear of second-placed Burnley and fifteen points ahead of third-placed Derby. The promotion run to the Premier League was becoming a steady coronation of champions as the King Power Stadium team could now fail to gain automatic promotion only if they suffered an unlikely collapse. Even Tykes boss Danny Wilson was in awe of Vardy and his prowess in front of goal, saying he wished he had him in his team and declaring out loud what most pundits and fans were now thinking: 'Leicester are the best team in this division by a country mile, in my opinion. They're class, they're a good team to watch and I'm slightly jealous in one respect because they've got some quality players there. It's coming together for them now. They're a Premier League team in waiting, it's only a matter of time.'

Jamie would score his sixteenth and final goal of what had been a triumphant season for him and Leicester, after they had both struggled in the run-in a year earlier, towards the end of March 2014. He opened the scoring with a tap-in, latching on to a cross, in the 1–1 draw at Blackburn. It was his sixth goal in as many games and extended City's unbeaten run to seventeen league games, and skipper Wes Morgan paid tribute to Vardy for refusing to give in when he hit a crisis the previous season. He said Jamie had shown how strong and determined a character he was and just how much he wanted to succeed and to be a great player. Morgan told the press after the draw, 'Jamie and I get on well and what I remember is him saying he wasn't sure about the situation he was in, and as a good friend and teammate I put an arm around him to reassure him. I said, "Persevere, and things will turn around." And, credit to the guy, that is what has happened. He never gives up and I'm delighted for him. He got one and he could have had two or three. He's quick and runs all day, works hard and is a great finisher. He has the confidence that comes with scoring goals and has shined all season. He is a fantastic player. This season no defence has been able to handle him. He has got us out of some sticky situations with his goals. I'm glad he is on my team.'

Leicester were almost there and Vardy was close to nailing his own ambition of playing for a Premier League team. The player and the club were finally promoted on Saturday, 5 April, after beating rivals Sheffield Wednesday 2–1 the night before and learning QPR had lost against Bournemouth.

Keeper Kasper Schmeichel outlined just what it meant when he told Sky Sports, 'Tonight we celebrate but everyone who knows the mentality of the team or the staff knows as soon as tonight's over we get back to work. We want to keep pushing on and we'll be back working hard ahead of Tuesday's game at home to Brighton. Then the real hard work starts to stay in the Premier League.'

He paid tribute to the efforts of his teammates and stressed just how important the goals of Vardy and David Nugent had been in making the difference between drawing games and winning, between earning one point and earning the full three. He went on to say, 'We've had belief all the way through the season. I think we can look back and see when we scored late goals and had that never-say-die attitude. That helped us immensely and it's testimony to the players and staff that everyone's worked really well together. It's a great day and I'm really, really delighted.'

Gary Lineker, arguably the club's most famous striker ever, added his own congratulations, tweeting, 'Leicester City are promoted to the Premier League. A sentence I've been waiting to say for 10 years.'

City would eventually end the season as Championship winners on 102 points, nine ahead of Burnley and seventeen ahead of Derby, finally putting to bed the misery from a year previous when they had lost to Watford in the play-offs.

There was one more honour for Jamie at the end of the season. He narrowly missed out on the Leicester Player of the Year award, which went to Danny Drinkwater, but won the club's Players' Player of the Year award. He picked up the award at the end of April 2014, and the club's official website marked the occasion with the following statement: 'Despite Jamie Vardy missing out on the Player of the Year award, he would not leave the event empty-handed however – City's 16-goal striker earning the vote of his peers to pick up the highly-respected Players' Player of the Year award. The former Fleetwood man has certainly found his feet at Championship level this season and has tormented defences up and down the country with his lightning pace.

'Along with strike partner David Nugent, the duo have forged one of the deadliest partnerships in the league, while there can be little doubt that Vardy has been one of City's most-improved players this season.'

That was an excellent summary of what had been an excellent season for the former non-league man. Jamie Vardy had won the respect of his colleagues and had finally made the big time of the Premier League. But, even then, he was busy setting himself a new target. He told friends he and his teammates would celebrate and have a good break in summer, relaxing on holiday with family and enjoying the time off. But then he would be back for pre-season training, when 'the hard work would really begin'. Never one to rest on his laurels, Jamie now wanted to prove he was one of the best strikers in the top flight – and to even get picked for England. In April 2014, that might have seemed a long-shot unless you knew how determined a character he was underneath that larking-about, Jack-the-lad persona he often put on when among his teammates. No, he was deadly serious underneath it all. Only the best would be good enough. And the boy from nowhere would be just that within another eighteen months. The best striker and the top goal scorer in English football's top flight.

CHAPTER FIVE

THE GREAT ESCAPE

As a reward for his excellent work during the previous season, Leicester offered Jamie Vardy a new contract in the first month of the new 2014–15 campaign. He had proved himself as a goalscorer and the club were keen to tie him down long-term. Gone were the depressing memories of that crisis in April 2013, when he had seriously considered quitting football. His efforts from August 2013 to April 2014 had shown he was over that dark period and all was well with his emotional wellbeing and his game. Sixteen goals was a fine riposte and City boss Nigel Pearson, who had been his biggest cheerleader, was convinced that the best was still to come; that Vardy would build on that promising contribution and deliver even more goals. Pearson wanted to ensure his 'pest' remained at the King Power – that no one would come in and poach his goal-poacher-in-chief.

The new four-year deal tied Jamie to the club until June 2018 and he told Leicester's official website, 'I'm over the moon. We all know that the club wants to keep improving and stay in the Premier League, and I definitely want to be a part of that. Everyone knows the way that I've come back into football [from non-league], and we managed to get promoted last season, but now it's all about making sure that we stay in the Premier League. Nigel Pearson brought me here and he wants the club to maintain their Premier League status. He was a big influence [on Jamie's signing a new deal] and now I've just got to repay him on the field.'

City's fans were just as delighted that Vardy was being looked after by the club. One commented, 'What a player, got pace, a quick change of acceleration, can take on defenders and has got a classic striker's finish. Formed a deadly partnership with Nugent last season, understood each other well. Plays a bit like Michael Owen in his prime.' And a footie fan in Fleetwood, from where Vardy was signed, added, 'I'm from Fleetwood and I've met the guy in a bar once. Had no idea who he was – just thought he was one of the lads. Then I saw him sign for Leicester on the news . . . top lad, good to see him doing well, a genuinely nice guy.'

The new deal was announced as Jamie was recovering from a thigh injury that would keep him out of the club's opening three fixtures of the new season – a 2–2 draw at home to Everton, a 2–0 defeat at Chelsea and a 1–0 loss at home to Shrewsbury in the Capital One Cup. He would eventually be fit for the final fixture of August, a 1–1 home draw with Arsenal. Jamie made his Premier League debut as a seventieth-minute substitute in the match at the King Power Stadium, and was thwarted from scoring a late winner only when Gunners keeper Wojciech Szczesny denied him with a fine save from a fizzing shot. Life in the top flight would be difficult for the Foxes and Vardy in the first half of the season. They got caught up in a relegation dogfight that was demanding, testing and disheartening.

It had also seemed unlikely after they put in a magnificent display against the mighty Manchester United on 21 September 2014, a display in which Vardy caught the eye and was unanimously applauded by fans, TV viewers and pundits as Man of the Match. It was Jamie's best performance of the season as he scored one goal and set up the other four for City as they came back from 3–1 down to beat United 5–3 at the King Power. It was certainly an impressive way to announce his arrival on the big stage and make headlines both in Britain and abroad, such was the prestige in Leicester putting five goals past one of the biggest clubs on the planet. The Fleet Street sports desks went Vardy crazy after his storming show, with *The Guardian* perhaps best summing up the general view: 'Jamie Vardy, who was playing for Stocksbridge Park Steels four years ago, in the eighth tier of English football, had the game of his life. The Leicester forward set up the first, won two penalties and scored the fourth. He even had a hand in Leicester's other goal, when Dean Hammond's shot struck him and bounced kindly for Esteban Cambiasso, on his first Premier League start, to make it 3–3. The Argentinian celebrated the goal as if it meant as much to him as any he scored for Internazionale.'

A young United central defender, Tyler Blackett, was dismissed for a professional foul on Vardy, as the striker's influence on the game knew no bounds. It was the performance of a man who had waited long enough to arrive on the world stage and who was now determined to make up for lost time. Jamie virtually destroyed Manchester United by himself and totally overshadowed their £59 million record signing, Angel di Maria. He showed just how good he was in front of goal when he calmly slotted the ball past United's world-class keeper David de Gea with ten minutes remaining, putting City 4–3 ahead at a critical stage of the match.

The Sun called Vardy's display 'the greatest afternoon of his footballing life', adding, 'His touch and finish into the bottom corner was coolness personified.

'Three years ago, Vardy was sent off for Fleetwood against Kidderminster in the Conference. Now he was enjoying his first Premier League goal and undoubtedly the greatest afternoon of his footballing life. As was this stadium.'

Vardy was buzzing after the game. This was what he had turned pro for – the adulation, the glory, the passion to work for the team and the result and the personal satisfaction of a performance that had outranked world-class players on the opposing team. Most people had expected Angel di Maria and Wayne Rooney to steal the show but it had been Vardy, the boy from non-league, who had the biggest impact on the game and the result. He had been involved in every goal and been a nightmare for United's harassed defenders with his pace, skill and coolness in front of goal. Poor Tyler Blackett would not forget his contest with Vardy in a hurry; he was young and would learn from his sending-off but would be scarred for some time to come by the skinning he had suffered at the hands of the Leicester number 9.

Jamie's boss Nigel Pearson was elated by his display: the boy was paying him back for the confidence he had shown in him, first with that £1 million fee and then when Vardy had suffered his crisis of confidence. Pearson believed that the best was yet to come from Jamie but felt that his team were making progress as they became acclimatised to the more demanding nature of the Premier League. He said, 'To gain back-to-back wins in the Premier League is never easy, especially if you are a newly promoted team. For us to win away at Stoke and then follow it up by beating one of the major forces in British football is very satisfying. When you add into that coming from 3–1 behind, it's testament not just to our quality, but also the spirit and self-belief.'

It seemed that nothing would hold Vardy and Leicester back now: they had shown just what they were capable of with the destruction of United, and their fans hoped this was the dawn of a major push to finish in at least the top ten of the Premier League. Everything appeared to be in place: the manager, the owners, the stadium, the regular support and the stars coming through, such as Vardy and Mahrez. If the team continued in this rich vein of form – which they had enjoyed as they stormed to become champions of the Championship – the future was surely bright, wasn't it? But life, and football, are rarely as simple and well ordered as that, and the rest of the first half of the season turned out to be a near disaster for Jamie and his teammates. By Saturday, 10 January 2015, Leicester stood at rock bottom of the Premier League with just seventeen points from twenty-one matches, and Vardy had not scored a goal since that win over Man United in September. Whereas a year previously they had been storming their way to the Championship title with goals galore, they were now anchored to the foot of the Premier table with seemingly no hope of salvation. In those twenty-one league games they had netted just twenty times and they had conceded thirty-three.

Little had changed by the end of February 2015, although, if anything, things had got worse. They were still bottom – with eighteen points from twenty-six games – and Jamie had still not found the net. And, a month later, they had picked up just one more point from three more games. City remained at rock bottom and lagged seven points behind Sunderland and safety. You would probably have bet your life savings on their being relegated; it was as near a certainty as one could imagine. They would need a miracle to stay up, but miracles rarely happened in life or football; league football was a long slog in which marathon runners often sagged and the eventual winners were those who paced themselves best over the full season. Same at the bottom of the pile: if your aim was pure survival you needed to pick up points here and there, but on a regular basis.

So the received wisdom was that the Foxes were indeed doomed; that they were on a fast boat back whence they came. To the Championship, regrouping and taking another pop at the big time when the boat had edged off the rocks and steadied. That would probably mean the sacking of Pearson and could even have meant a fire sale of their most saleable assets, even including Jamie Vardy. His Leicester dream might have ended there.

Yet one month later, at the end of April 2015, Leicester had dragged themselves out of the drop zone and had accumulated twelve points from seven games. They were now a point clear of Sunderland, who had fallen to third bottom, and had a much better goal difference. It was an escape act worthy of Houdini at his unbelievable best.

But not only was it an escape worthy of a movie, it became a case of watching a team play to its potential, and beyond. For in the four remaining games of the campaign City amassed ten points, which left them in fourteenth place with forty-one, four places and six points clear of the drop zone.

It was title-winning form. To highlight just how massive a turnaround it was, title winners Chelsea took just seven points from their final four games.

And it was clear that Leicester and Vardy had turned a corner. Self-belief and a willingness to play to their maximum had returned at just the right time. After that early-season win over Man United, Vardy had collected more yellow cards than goals – six yellows, no goals – from 21 September 2014 up until 21 March 2015. But there were stirrings of a return to form for him and the team on that March afternoon. Okay, they lost 4–3 at Tottenham but the gulf had closed. It had been a loss by one goal and Jamie had finally ended his goal drought. He pulled a goal back when it was 2–0 to Spurs, neatly finishing after a smart pass from Nugent. Okay, he was overshadowed by Harry Kane, the hosts' striker who would eventually battle him for an England starting role, who grabbed a brilliant hat-trick.

But I believe his own and Leicester's renaissance began that day in north London. The shadows of doubt and negativity were slowly dispersing to be replaced by a vibrancy and that fantastic self-belief. It is a telling statistic that, after that defeat at White Hart Lane, City went on a run that saw them win seven, draw one and lose just one (and that against eventual champs Chelsea) of their remaining nine Premier League games that season. And Vardy's own stats improved dramatically, considering he had not scored for almost six months.

After netting at Tottenham, he now notched three more goals in the season's last few weeks, and contributed to several others to help his team to safety. He scored the decisive goal in a 3–2 win at Midlands rivals West Brom on 11 April, and the winner at Burnley a fortnight later. The winner at West Brom sent the City fans and boss Pearson wild and it was a goal that Jamie will never forget, especially as he had so much work to do to score it. He took the ball off a napping Albion play on the halfway line, sped towards goal, beat another defender and then finished brilliantly, firing home past the hapless keeper. It was the goal of a man determined to prove he still had what it takes to be a top player – and a man determined to keep his team up, and his boss in a job.

It was little wonder, then, that Pearson singled him out after the match, telling reporters, 'It was an exceptional goal from Jamie Vardy but we can't get carried away. It's great to get back-to-back wins but we still have an awful lot to do. We have had some occasions of late, especially in away games, where we don't feel we have had things go our way. It's nice to make things go our way. The players were frustrated with themselves in the first half. We didn't quite get going. We gave a side who looked to be a little nervy themselves a little cushion.'

Jamie scored his final goal that season in the final match as City crushed QPR 5–1 at the King Power Stadium. It helped him celebrate his first call-up to the England squad, which in itself was a surprise to many. They wondered how his call-up was justified when he had struggled for many months until hitting form at the end of March. The clue was in the last part of the last sentence: he had hit form recently and that was enough for England boss Roy Hodgson and many more, including myself, who had never really doubted the boy's potential or talent. Along with Harry Kane, he was the England striker on the best form at that particular time of the season, and that was what counted. He had shown he could cut it with the best, and this was his reward.

Nigel Pearson also realised the contribution Jamie had made to his own future and the club's Premier League survival by substituting him on sixty-five minutes, after he had put the Foxes 1–0 ahead against QPR. He wasn't injured: it was Pearson's way of thanking him. As Jamie went off, he got a standing ovation from the Leicester faithful, who were also well aware of his efforts – and of what he could do the next season if he hit form. Pearson said later, 'His England call-up reflects his own performances but also [the] fact he is playing in a side which has taken the eye. I'm delighted for him.'

Vardy had snapped up one of his typical poacher goals, being the first to react when Mahrez's shot was parried by the keeper and slotting the ball home calmly. Afterwards Pearson hugged Vardy and the rest of his players and thanked them as a group and individually for their Herculean end-of-season efforts. He then told the press, 'We took a bit of time to get going. It is always difficult when you've achieved certain objectives to get what you want. The end product is a really good win, but we didn't quite hit some of the standards we would have liked, but we did more than enough in the end. It was a shame it wasn't a clean sheet as well as a win. But there are lots of positives and it's always important to try and finish a season with an outcome you can build on for next year. We are not kidding ourselves in terms of how we need to move forward, because, although it has been a great end to the season, it needed to be.'

Yes, it was certainly a case of relief and hope after a season that had been, for the most part, a mighty struggle for both the manager and his players. Vardy and City had survived but five goals in thirty-four Premier League appearances that season hardly suggested Jamie would be headline news the next campaign. They gave no hint of the remarkable goals record he would embark upon – there again, who would have bet on the likelihood of Nigel Pearson getting the sack and being replaced by Claudio Ranieri and that change working out so fantastically well, with Leicester top of the league for most of the following season? Football, eh? Bloody hell, as the great Sir Alex Ferguson once commented.

CHAPTER SIX

IN THE FOOTSTEPS OF LEGENDS

Jamie Vardy wasn't the first Foxes striker to make a massive impact at club and international level. There were similarities with the man who remains, arguably, Leicester's greatest forward player: Gary Lineker, now firmly ensconced in his role as *Match of the Day* host. Both Jamie and Gary were swift of mind and deed in front of the goal and both emerged after a slow start at Leicester. Both were foxes in the box and both were fast and incredibly difficult to stay with, let alone stop, when in full motion. And both had an eye for a goal that developed and was immaculate when fully realised. These facts make a more thorough comparison worthwhile and we will deal with these fully in the next chapter.

But, before we move on to the Lineker link and then on to that record-breaking goals season, let's pause a moment and examine how Vardy was walking – nay, running – in the footsteps of legends. There were, of course, other Leicester strikers through the ages who demand more than a mere mention when putting Jamie's remarkable 2015–16 achievements into perspective.

Frank Worthington, for example, certainly made his mark at the then Filbert Street ground in the 1970s and earned the accolade of runner-up in the club's greatest players of all time, just behind Lineker, on the fansite *Foxes Talk*. 'Elvis', as he was fondly known due to his slicked-back hair and tendency to wear the tightest of trousers, was more flamboyant on and off the pitch than Vardy or Lineker. He was perhaps a more stylish player in the sense that he strutted around as if he owned the place and his goals were usually more distinctive efforts – more memorable in their execution.

I met Worthington just the once – at Leeds's Elland Road ground, but not on a footballing occasion. We were both present at the end of May in 1982 to watch the rock band Queen perform at the stadium. My recollection is that Frank was a fun guy, certainly noticeable in black leather trousers and that slicked-backed hair, and he liked a joke and a laugh. The ladies flocked around him and he certainly lived up to his reputation as a man who loved a glass or two in the VIP lounge!

He surprised me by proving not to be a prima donna – just a down-to-earth guy who liked Elvis and rock 'n' roll and to have a good time, which he certainly had at Leeds that day, both in the bar and in the stands, as Freddie Mercury and the boys belted out their innumerable hits.

As a player, Worthy was a stroller and a crowd pleaser with

his silky skills, Leicester's answer to Stan Bowles and Tony Currie. Again, that marked him out as a very different beast from Jamie and Lineker, who were much more the predator than the show pony. Not that old Worthy put the showing-off before scoring goals – his record of one goal roughly every three games at Filbert Street showed just how good a striker he was. He hit a total of seventy-two in 210 games for the Foxes in a five-year period from 1972 to 1977, and enjoyed his best footballing days at the club. Indeed, his eight England appearances, with two goals to show, were claimed in 1974 at the peak of his career at Leicester.

Worthy looked the part, with his socks more often than not rolled down to his ankles, his shirt out of his shorts and his long locks flowing in the wind. He was a showman, no doubt about that. And, like Bowles and Currie, a maverick, too – and the fans loved him all the more for that, although it did sometimes bring him into conflict with football managers. Frank would win just eight caps for England when he surely deserved many more, given his talent. But Don Revie, the then England boss, wasn't a fan. Frank recalled, 'He wanted the yes-men. He didn't like the individuals, the characters, the rebels.'

On the other side of the coin, Alan Birchenall, a former teammate at Filbert Street, told *The Huddersfield Daily Examiner* how Frank reacted when he was appreciated – as he was under Jimmy Bloomfield at Leicester. Alan said, 'Under Jimmy, Elvis was magnificent, but a law unto himself. Most of the time, you just left him to do what he wanted. These days players are out on the pitch well in advance of kick-off, but Frank would often report to the ground at 2 p.m., then disappear for half an hour! More often than not he'd be signing autographs in the car park or grabbing the numbers of some admiring females! I also remember times on the training ground when we would be getting a roasting while Frank would be at the other end, volleying in shots that one of the youth team players was setting up for him. The coach just left Frank to it!'

In his entertaining autobiography *One Hump or Two?* Frank expounded upon his own views about England and the game in general. He said, 'I've no time for England managers like Don Revie and Graham Taylor. They just seemed determined to squeeze out individual flair. I hope England can find a role for players like Matthew Le Tissier . . . [and] there just don't seem to be the characters about today. In my day there were big personalities at every club. I think back to people like Tony Currie, Alan Birchenall, Rodney Marsh, Mike Summerbee and Alan Hudson. The list is endless. I think there is too much money in the game now as well. I know it's a short career but the superstars are greedy.'

Frank's own skill level often left opponents for dead – and just as often wanting to punch his lights out! Frank recalled how he once left Johnny Giles of Leeds looking a fool with a particular piece of skill, and how Giles threatened to get his own back. Frank explained, 'I was down by the corner flag and flipped the ball over my shoulder and over his head. He just turned to me and said, in a cold, calculating, matter-of-fact sort of way, "If you ever take the piss out of me or Leeds United again, I'll break your legs."'

For all his laid-back approach, Frank could be just as growly as Vardy over perceived, or real, lack of effort or talent, if he felt his teammates at Leicester were not pulling their weight. In September 1976, after a 2–2 draw with QPR in the old English First Division, he told reporters, 'People are always telling me there's a lot of skill in our side. You tell me where it is. There are one or two skilful players, and that's it. The rest are workers.'

And the Leicester fans will always have a place in their hearts for Frank. One fan said, 'Frank was a legend at Filbert Street – what wage would he be getting in this day and age? Characters such of the likes of Worthington and the late great Keith Weller will not be seen ever again. All clubs have their legends and Frank was one at Leicester.'

That he still managed to strike the balance between show and results is testament to his love of the game and his talent as a centre-forward. When the *Leicester Mercury* carried out a series of pieces to find the ultimate City XI, it was of little surprise, therefore, that Worthy found a place upfront, as one of the three strikers. And the paper described his selection in these glowing – and deserved – terms: 'The first spot in our front three goes to the man they call "Elvis". Worthington was the first name out of all the judges' mouths. The superstar of Jimmy Bloomfield's skilful side of the 70s, he was a genius with the football. He embodied the elegant flair, arrogance and flamboyance that accompanied him off the pitch as well as on it.'

Frank would be the first to concede he lived life to the full away from the game – although he always took his football seriously. In 1985, he told the *Daily Express*, 'I have not been an angel, but nothing has ever come before football. I have no complaints about my life and my career so far . . . I have never made excuses for anything because that is a weakness. I have always known what I was about and where I was going.'

Frank left Leicester in 1977 for Bolton and was the First Division's leading goalscorer in the 1978–9 campaign with a total of twenty-four. That haul included what many pundits claim to be his greatest goal – when he scored in the 3–2 defeat to Ipswich in April 1979. Frank controlled the ball with his head, juggled it twice with his left foot, flicked it over his shoulder and then fired home. It was a goal that Vardy would most certainly have been proud of. Bolton had splashed out a then-club-record £90,000 fee – an illustration of his worth – and most Leicester fans were sorry to see him go. Frank had provided them with many moments of joy and flair and had lit up Filbert Street with his positive play.

The *Leicester Mercury*'s next choice in that all-time front three was a man whose goalscoring exploits Jamie Vardy would dearly love to emulate – and who certainly merits a mention in Leicester's all-time-greats portfolio. It's Arthur Rowley, the all-time top scorer in the English Football League. Rowley hit an incredible 434 goals in 619 league games – with 251 coming at Leicester in 303 league games from 1950 to 1958. The man nicknamed 'The Gunner', because of his explosive left foot, holds the record for the most goals in a single season at the club, with forty-four in forty-two league matches in 1956–7.

He is also the Foxes' second all-time top goalscorer, netting 265 times in 321 league and cup games, just eight short of

Arthur Chandler. Similar to Jamie and Lineker, Rowley had a slow start in the goalscoring stakes at the club, but when he finally did find the net, like the latter-day duo, they didn't stop coming and he ended up with twenty-eight in his first season. Rowley liked his hat-tricks, too, notching a total of sixteen.

His standing with the fans could be seen by the fact that, when manager Dave Halliday sold him to Shrewsbury in 1958, the fans rebelled and the manager was sacked.

Vardy learned of Rowley's feats at the end of October 2015, when he surpassed another of Arthur's records. His seventy-seventh-minute goal in a 3–2 win at West Brom meant that Jamie had scored in eight consecutive games for the Foxes, beating the all-time Leicester record of seven in seven achieved by Rowley and another hero of a bygone era, Chandler.

And the greatest compliment I could pay to Jamie is that his feat surprised no one – in fact, most commentators expected him to beat Rowley's achievement, even though it is probably harder to score goals in the modern game, given the increased tactical emphasis. Even the bookies had Jamie odds-on to surpass Rowley. Betfred had said beforehand, 'England international Vardy is the top scorer in the Premier League this season with seven from eight games, a ratio that puts him in with a chance of overtaking the record of the great Rowley who scored 44 times in 42 league games for the Foxes in 1956–57 season.

'That is 28-year-old Vardy's long term target, but more immediately on his radar is Rowley's club record of scoring in seven consecutive league matches which he achieved in that same goal-crazy season 58 years ago.'

Of course, Jamie did exceed that record – and then moved some beyond it, too.

The aforementioned Arthur Chandler starred as a striker for Leicester in the period 1923–35 and remains their all-time top scorer with 273 goals in 419 appearances. Chandler, who had a suite named after him at the club, is rated among the greats by Leicester club historian, John Hutchinson, who had this to say about the player: 'When "Channy" signed for Leicester City in 1923 he was already nearly twenty-eight. Up until then, he had only scored eighteen goals for QPR in the old Third Division South. Once he arrived at Filbert Street, the picture changed dramatically.

'An ever-present in his first two seasons at Leicester, he scored sixty-one league and cup goals, culminating in Leicester becoming Second Division Champions in 1925. He then scored 212 league and cup goals in the next ten seasons, by which time he was nearly forty. He scored 154 of them in the first five seasons in First Division. He scored thirty-four goals in 1928–9, when Leicester came within a point of winning the league title.

'He also scored a phenomenal thirty-three goals in sixteen games on the FA tour to South Africa in 1929. In addition, he scored in all three of his England trials.

'His final tally of 273 goals in 419 games, including seventeen hat-tricks, is still a Club record. Arthur left Filbert Street for a brief spell at Notts County in 1935, before joining Leicester's backroom staff, where he served in various capacities until he retired in 1969, aged seventy-three.'

Mr Hutchinson also mentioned the famous 'Six Swans' game – in which Chandler grabbed a double hat-trick. Leicester beat Portsmouth 10–0 in October 1928 with Chandler on the rampage. Five swans flew overhead after Arthur grabbed his fifth goal and his sixth arrived just as another swan flew by!

On a level just below the two Arthurs and Worthington are the likes of Alan Smith, Emile Heskey and Allan Clarke. Of the three, Clarke was arguably the best, but he only really realised his full potential when he moved to Leeds in 1969. Signed from Fulham a year earlier, he made thirty-six appearances for the Foxes and scored a creditable twelve goals. Clarke had a languid, laid-back style but was deadly in front of goal. He also made a major contribution to Leicester's FA Cup final run in his year at the club, scoring the winner in the 1969 semi-final against West Brom. Allan played well in the final at Wembley but was unable to help the Foxes from slipping to a 1–0 defeat to Manchester City, with Neil Young firing home a memorable winner.

At Leeds, Clarke would earn the moniker 'Sniffer', because he was the master of sniffing out goals in the penalty box, would form a fine partnership with Mick Jones and would play a key role in Leeds's domination of the league and for England at national level.

Alan Smith, meanwhile, would enjoy a fuller career at Filbert Street, staying with the club for five years from 1982 to 1987 and grabbing eighty-four goals in 200 games. But, like Clarke, he would cement his reputation away from the club. Smith left for Arsenal in 1987 and made 347 appearances, scoring 115 goals in an eight-year spell. Notably, Smith played upfront with

Lineker in his first season at the Foxes, scoring thirteen goals as they won promotion to the First Division.

Smith would also follow in Gary's footsteps when he hung up his boots, moving into television as an analyst for Sky Sports and proving himself very adept at the role with succinct and telling comments during and after matches in the top flight.

In 2001, Smith told reporters of his joy when he became a pro and how tough it was when he was forced out of the game through injury. He said, 'I became a professional footballer in 1982 when I joined Leicester City. Played for them for five years. I think I scored seventy-six goals for them in that time. And then I joined Arsenal in 1987 for £750,000. We were lucky enough to win the league in 1989. Arsenal hadn't won it in eighteen years. I won the golden boot that season as the division's top scorer, then we won the league again in '91 and a few more trophies came and I retired in 1995 after a bad knee injury.'

He was then asked by the BBC what he believed makes a top striker – and his analysis could have been an identikit for the player Jamie Vardy has become.

Smith said, 'He's got to be single-minded if he wants to score goals. There were times where perhaps there might a better pass on but you see the goals and you want to have a shot. I wasn't a particularly selfish type of striker: I was more of a team player. I never regarded myself as an out-and-out goal scorer but you've got to have that single-minded side to your character. You've got to be a good footballer, have good control, all the normal things that you would expect to become a footballer. But being a striker is quite a specialised job and a lot of it is mental – having the confidence and self-belief to go out there and knock them in. Sometimes chances can look easy, but when you're not in a run of good form they're very difficult.'

Yes, Smith could certainly have been describing Jamie, given the boy's totally focused attitude and determination to make the top grade against the odds. And the analysis that self-belief is a key element also applies to Jamie, who never doubted he was good enough. He just needed a big break and when it came he took his chance hungrily.

Emile Heskey is also a striker who has a place in the hearts of many Leicester fans. The big man provided the ideal foil for Michael Owen and then Wayne Rooney when he played for England. He even admitted that one of, if not the, most memorable of his goals came for England, when they crushed Germany 5–1 in Munich in September 2001. Emile told Goal. com, 'I don't know if it's the best goal but the one everyone remembers is in the 5–1 against Germany. It's not the best I've scored, but that's the one I'll always be remembered for. We didn't realise until the final whistle and we got in the changing rooms what we'd actually done. Collectively we'd played a massive game, and you've got to remember we were down 1–0 after eight minutes. It could have been two. We galvanised ourselves and were lucky enough to have Michael Owen and his goalscoring ability, and I managed to score as well. It was a great performance for us and the fans that travelled.'

And unlike the two Alans, Clarke and Smith, Emile spent

the best days of his career at Leicester. He played for the club from 1994 to 2000, making 154 appearances and scoring forty goals. Not renowned for his goals returns – especially on England duty, when he scored just seven in sixty-two games – his record of one in four at Leicester is not to be sniffed at. And he also weighed in with many assists and help for the goal aces who played in attack with him. His physique and presence created plenty of space for others to cash in, as he opened up defences and frightened his opponents with his sheer physicality and strength.

Heskey was born in Leicester and grew up there, winning a place at City's academy when he was just nine. Progressing through the youth and reserve team ranks, he made his first team debut at the age of seventeen in a Premier League clash against QPR in 1995. Quickly, he established his place in the first team, helping the club to win promotion back to the Premier League after they were relegated. In the 1995–6 campaign he netted ten times for the club in thirty-five games and scored a vital goal in the League Cup final the following season.

Leicester had been losing 1–0 to Middlesbrough after a Fabrizio Ravanelli goal at Wembley and were heading for defeat when Heskey rescued the day, equalising in the very last minute of extra time. Afterwards, Emile admitted, 'It is the most important goal I've ever scored.'

Boro boss and former Manchester United great Bryan Robson admitted Heskey's goal had left him 'gutted', adding, 'I am desperately disappointed, as I really thought we had the game under control in the extra period. Ravanelli scored a great goal but could have had a hat-trick. Leicester defended well. They made it very difficult for us, as I'm sure they will do next time. Yet I still believe we can lift this trophy.'

Leicester boss Martin O'Neill hailed 'hero' Emile and added, 'The effort of my lads was fantastic. Middlesbrough have world-class players, but we refused to be overawed. Sure, I am optimistic about the replay.'

He was right to be optimistic, as the Foxes now went on to win the League Cup by virtue of a 1–0 win at Hillsborough, Sheffield. Heskey's attacking partner Steve Claridge scored the goal that brought the trophy back to Leicester.

Heskey spoke of his joy that he had won a trophy with his hometown club and City boss Martin O'Neill paid tribute to his 'hard work' and 'selfless' efforts.

The brilliant win also meant Leicester would embark upon major European competition for only the second time in their history. The bookies had them at 60–1 to win the UEFA Cup but that didn't worry Emile and co. They were simply delighted to be in the competition.

Heskey spoke of his 'pride' at representing his hometown in Europe and midfielder Garry Parker was also optimistic, saying, 'A lot of teams have been disappointing in Europe, but we're a hard-working team and will give it our best shot. We are a hard team to beat. We work for each other and we'll just see what happens. But Leicester in Europe? Who would have believed it at the start of the season?'

Claridge, like Heskey and Parker, also had to pinch himself to believe he would be playing in Europe. He said, 'A lot of people thought I was more likely to end up on a park bench than in Europe. There have been a lot of times when I have been tempted to pack it in, but I stuck at it because I love the buzz of scoring goals.'

Ironically, Leicester were paired with crack Spanish outfit Atlético Madrid in the first round in 1997 – the same team they had lost 3–1 to thirty-six years earlier in the second round of the European Cup Winners' Cup.

Once again, the Spaniards would triumph – this time with an aggregate 4–1 win.

Heskey left Leicester for Liverpool in 2000 for a fee of £11 million. But he would always admit City was his main love and in 2014 said how he would love to return to the club for a final hurrah. Then thirty-six years old, and a free agent after a two-year spell in Australia, Emile revealed his continuing, lifelong affection for his hometown team. He told BBC Radio Leicester, 'It goes without saying, I'd love to come back to Leicester. It is a great club that allowed me to get to the platform that I got to. I was an England international when I was with Leicester so that was a great achievement.'

At the time the Foxes were struggling at the foot of the Premier League but Heskey was convinced he could guide them to safety, saying, 'They have got a decent squad there, they just need that little pick-me-up, a little confidence. It could be anything, just a spark to get going on a run to get out of it.'

Unfortunately for Emile, it wasn't to be – and it was probably for the best as many fans did not back the idea. *Metro* writer and Leicester fan Chris Forryan summed up the gamble that bringing Heskey back would have been – even while admitting Heskey was one of his footballing heroes. He said, 'Nigel Pearson is putting together a young squad (shown by the development squad's European adventures) and, whilst the odd old head is good to have around, we have David Nugent on the field and Kevin Phillips off it that fall into this category.

'However, in a poll on social media more than 30 per cent of Fox fans disagree and think we should let Emile boot up again. Leicester City could well become a laughing stock if this rumour becomes reality. And if it didn't work out a man seen as a hero to many could soon lose that crown. It is obvious to even the bluest of blue fans that something needs to be done and the addition of new players come January looks a necessity but Emile, I would venture, should not be one of them.'

Sure, the fans had enjoyed and loved Heskey at his peak, but he was well past it by that stage in 2014 and could have spoiled the fond memories he and those loyal supporters had of his time at the club.

What's more, Leicester boss Nigel Pearson was also not keen on a potential Heskey return. He said, 'You're reading a bit too much into it to suggest he would improve what we've got here at the minute.'

And, of course, if Emile had returned he could have stunted the growth of the club's other forwards, including Vardy. Instead, the club would use Heskey in an ambassadorial role, whereby he would work with their Thailand International Academy and would also be an honorary ambassador for the Foxes Foundation charity.

Fortunately, Emile was ultimately more than happy to fulfil that role for the club, even when his dream of returning as a player was dashed. He told the press, 'Leicester City is where it all started for me, so it is with great pride that I return to the club in a role I am really excited about. Coming up through the club's academy and developing into a first-team footballer were some of the most important years of my career, but they were also some of the most enjoyable.

'My aim is to help these young players to have a similar experience while they are studying and playing in Leicester. I owe so much to Leicester City and to the education I received in the club's academy, so I'm delighted to be able to give something back at the other end of my career.'

Another Foxes striker hero who also did his fair bit in helping youngsters through to the first team was Septimus 'Sep' Smith, who starred for the club for twenty years, from 1929 to 1949. He is often spoken of as Leicester's all-time-best all-round player, and he merits inclusion here because he did play upfront as well as in midfield. His unusual name originated from the fact that he was the seventh son born in his family in Whitburn, Co. Durham. He also holds the record of being the club's longest-serving player and the longest-serving skipper (thirteen years).

He was a prolific scorer for the reserves and soon earned a regular first-team place in the 1931–2 season, when he netted once every two games in twenty-two matches. Smith made it his business to bring younger players through the ranks. One such player was the future Leeds and England boss Don Revie, whom we have already mentioned in this chapter. Smith said of Revie, 'I could see that he had potential when he came down for a trial and I used to coach him lots with the ball. I would say come with me, and we would go into a corner and I'd teach him things. He was an eager young player but I used to make him cry when I told him he did things wrong. He told me he would go home after the match and start to cry. I was pushing him because I believed in him. When he used to cry, I told him he should do things right. But he could cross a ball and kick a ball the right way. I would teach him the way to go . . . to pass the ball in front of the player so he could run on to it. And I would teach him how to trap it.'

In turn, Revie dedicated a chapter, 'What I Owe to Sep Smith', to him in his 1955 autobiography, *Soccer's Happy Wanderer*, saying, 'I'm proud now to think of how much time Sep spent passing on his soccer knowledge to me. He played a big part in my shaping my career. He could place the ball within an inch of a man's toe . . . and when he lobbed the ball to his winger the opposing full-back felt the ball graze his hair as he tried to strain his neck that extra inch, like a drowning man trying to lift his head out of the water.'

Smith certainly deserves his mention in this chapter as we analyse the predecessors to Jamie Vardy who illuminated Leicester's history. How important – and valued – Sep was and remains to the club is illustrated by his being the guest of honour at the final game at Filbert Street in April 2002 and that a suite at the King Power Stadium is named in his honour. Jamie would have to maintain his incredible scoring feats for many more seasons to earn the right for his named suite! Sep died on 28 July 2006, at the age of ninety-four, and a minute's silence was held in his memory at Leicester's next game as the crowd paid tribute as one to the man who contributed so much for the club he loved.

It was a fitting and moving salute. Sep Smith was a true great, as were Frank Worthington, Arthur Rowley and Arthur Chandler. Like Emile Heskey and Alan Smith, he contributed much colour and depth to Leicester City's illustrious history – just as Jamie Vardy is doing right now.

Now let's turn our attentions to the man who arguably most resembles Vardy as a striker in the club's annals – the King of the Crisps and Goals: Gary Lineker.

CHAPTER SEVEN

THE LINEKER LINK

Whenever Jamie Vardy's impact at the King Power Stadium is discussed, the talk invariably turns to comparisons with the man many Leicester fans consider their greatest striker, Gary Lineker. Unlike that of the majority of the other City forwards we have focused on in the previous chapter – Emile Heskey, Frank Worthington and Alan Smith, for instance – Vardy's talent is not that of a big target man or a showman centre-forward. No, his particular worth centres on his instinctive ability to latch onto a ball in the box and to bury it. He is a natural 'fox in the box' but can just as easily beat a man outside with his speed and hammer the ball home. In this respect, he is the modern-day version of Lineker.

Those attributes enabled Jamie to notch up that wonderful, consecutive-games goalscoring record, beating the efforts of former Manchester United striker Ruud van Nistelrooy. It is also no coincidence that the Dutchman himself was famed for scoring the majority of *his* goals in the penalty area, either. But that didn't mean – like Jamie – that Ruud's goals were any less worthy, or that he never scored *great* goals.

As Sam Wallace, writing in *The Independent* in 2010, pointed out, '[Cristiano] Ronaldo scored 118 goals in 292 games for United, averaging one every 2.8 games compared to Van Nistelrooy's average of one every 1.46 games. Van Nistelrooy, a poacher, was not as exciting or original as Ronaldo, but for four of his five years his contribution was just as crucial. [Ruud] famously never scored a goal hit from outside the box for United, although that wrongly suggests he never scored spectacular goals. The second goal in his hat-trick against Fulham in March 2003 began in his own half and took him past four Fulham defenders before he scored from close range. His second goal against Basle in November 2002 wasn't too shabby either.'

And *The Daily Telegraph* pointed out that, by the end of November 2015, only three of the combined 113 league goals Jamie and Ruud had scored in the English top flight had come from outside the area.

Lineker, too, was a six-yard-box predator – and almost a prototype for Vardy. It was Leicester's great fortune that they would find a player equally as deadly thirty years after Gary was filling his boots at Filbert Street. Vardy has picked up the mantle for Leicester that Lineker abdicated when he moved to Everton in 1985, two years before Jamie was born.

If they were similar creatures in the penalty area, they differed in other aspects. While Jamie is very much a late bloomer in football's big time, Gary was schooled for stardom from an early age. Born in Leicester in November 1960, he was destined for the top when he signed schoolboy forms with City, his hometown club. Lineker's links with his hometown would make it all the harder for the fans to swallow when he eventually decided to leave for Goodison Park in the mid-1980s. He had grown up in the city, gone to local primary and high schools and played football with his older brother Wayne. His dad was a well-known greengrocer in Leicester, as the business had been around for decades.

And, unlike Vardy, he had other sporting strings to his bow. While Jamie focused solely on his football, Gary was also a talented cricketer and maybe could have made the grade there, too. He was the skipper of the Leicestershire Schools team and even thought at one stage that he could follow a career in cricket. And, when he looked back on his life in March 2010, he admitted he would also probably have tried harder in his school subjects if he had known that the competition to make the grade as a footballer was going to be so tough.

Gary told *The Independent*, 'If I'd known how difficult it was to be a footballer, I would have worked harder at school. I did okay, but my mind was elsewhere. My last report said something along the lines of: "He concentrates far too much on football. He'll never make a living at that." These were wise words in many ways; a huge percentage of boys don't make a living at it.

'When you do well at one sport, you tend to do well at other sports. I was in both the football and cricket teams and got a lot of goals and runs. I was captain of the Leicestershire Schools cricket team from 11 to 16 and thought at the time I would probably have more chance afterwards in cricket than football.'

Gary may have thought he had it tough – but his progress was garlanded in comparison with Jamie's. Where Jamie had to battle every step of the way for acceptance on the pro footballing ladder, Gary's steps were almost preordained. He would become a player for his local team after being spotted by the club as a thirteen-year-old. That led him into the Leicester youth academy and, at the age of sixteen, he started to play full-time after leaving school. Not for him the life of graft outside the game – while still trying to gain a foothold within the game itself – that Jamie faced. Gary could conceivably have ended up in the grocery business like his father, grandfather and great-grandfather.

That said, full credit to Gary for his dedication to becoming a pro footballer. As he expressed in his comments to *The Independent*, it was no easy ride and he could just as easily have been on the scrapheap that beckons for many hopefuls. His hard work and Leicester's ongoing belief that he could make it are commendable. By the age of eighteen, Gary was playing for the Foxes' first team and on the ladder that would rise to the heights of his becoming England's top all-time goalscorer (until Wayne Rooney surpassed his record).

Gary made his debut for Leicester on New Year's Day 1979 in the 2–0 home victory against Oldham Athletic. In common with Vardy, he had pace galore and initially it was to his detriment, as Leicester played him on the right wing. They felt that turn of speed could leave opponents for dead and set up chances for the hitmen in the middle. Of course, there was substance in that view, but it failed to take into account the player's natural instinct in front of goal.

When he was given a chance as an out-and-out striker it was quickly apparent that Lineker's pace could be a massive plus in that role. He was good on the wing but he was better as a predator in the six-yard area. Later in his career, at Barcelona, Gary would also be played out of position on the wing by Johan Cruyff, a blunder by the Dutch legend. Was Cruyff trying to make the point that he was the boss now after Terry Venables had left the Camp Nou – and Lineker would suffer by association?

Possibly. But, if so, it was a foolish 'cut off your nose off to spite your face' sort of decision by Cruyff, since it deprived him of a natural scorer who had become a hero of the Barça fans after helping the club lift the Spanish Cup.

Like Vardy, Lineker started slowly at Leicester, taking time to find his feet and to regularly hit the goal trail. In his debut season, 1978–9, he made eight appearances, including one as a sub, but found the net just six times in thirty-five league games over three seasons. But, when the dam broke, the floodgates opened. By 1981 he was a regular starter in the team and he hit nineteen goals in all competitions in the 1981–2 season, firing the Foxes to the semi-finals of the 1982 FA Cup. Lineker scored in the 5–2 quarter-final win over Shrewsbury, an extraordinary match that saw injured Foxes keeper Mark Wallington concede twice before finally going off. In those days, there were no sub keepers, and so centre-forward Alan Young took his place between the sticks. By half-time it was two apiece in the goal stakes, but then, remarkably, Young also got injured, so Foxes' stand-in keeper had to be replaced by a stand-in, stand-in keeper in Steve Lynex! As only one sub was allowed, Leicester were down to ten men, but Young eventually came back on and went back in goal, with Lynex moving out to the wing. It was a true comedy of errors, with the Foxes ripping up the script that should have seen them struggle with ten men for a time and incompetent keepers. But they managed not only to survive, but to thrive, running out comprehensive victors, with Gary making it 4–2 and a Jim Melrose goal cementing the win.

Like Gary, the fans also loved the match against Shrewsbury and the win notched up against the odds. One fan, DPJ, said, 'I am old enough, indeed was there at the Shrewsbury game in '82. We had three different goalkeepers – in the days before substitute keepers. Certainly, a game I will never forget. I live close to one of the Shrewsbury players on duty that day, Dave Tonge, and I remind him every time I see him! Happy days.'

Happy days indeed, and all part of the legacy Lineker was starting to create for himself as, like Vardy, he now hit the goal trail for the Foxes. In 2013, Steve Lynex would tell the *Leicester Mercury* that the match was one of his favourites, too, in the days when he played wide to provide the balls for Lineker. He also revealed that it was Gary's unbending will to succeed that particularly impressed him.

Lynex said, 'I had loads of great memories at City. Obviously, the Shrewsbury game was a memorable moment, when I had to go in goal, but we had promotions and relegations. It was a roller-coaster ride, but an enjoyable one. We played some great football in those days and it was very good for me as a winger. We had Gary Lineker coming through at the time and it was obvious that he would go on to become a top striker. He had the confidence, and, when he missed a few, his head never went down. He was always there for the next one. You have to give him credit for that, because a lot of guys would disappear.'

Lynex pointed out that he had been part of a forward line – along with Gary and Alan Smith – that had finished as the top scorers in the top flight in one of his seasons at the club. And, even though the 1982 FA campaign ended in a 2–0 semi-final defeat at the hands of Tottenham, it was an effort he and Lineker would never forget, especially after the Shrewsbury dramas, as they just missed out on a Wembley final appearance.

Lineker's most productive league season at Filbert Street came in the 1982–3 campaign, when his goals helped the club win promotion to the First Division. He scored twenty-six in forty matches, to take Leicester back into the top flight. It was not his best in terms of overall goals, as he failed to hit the net in both the FA and League Cups, thus ending the campaign with that twenty-six total. Gary's haul included two hat-tricks – against Carlisle and Derby – and five braces.

Gordon Milne had taken the club up to the top flight after replacing Jock Wallace as boss the previous summer. It is interesting to hear what he had to say about the fledgling talent Lineker was at the time – how Milne felt he struggled to keep his balance and how the manager knew straightaway that Gary, like Vardy, was going to be a 'fox-in-the-box' star. Milne told the *FoxBlog* in 2007: 'Well he [Lineker] was just beginning really. The thing that first struck me about him was that he used to fall over a lot. Every time he turned his legs would get tangled up and over he'd go. It was a case of working on his control, because that was a bit loose and a ball played into him could pop off him. In his make-up then that world-class player was in there, but we had to work on making him a part of a team. Smudger [Alan Smith] was better at keeping the ball and holding it up, he had a good touch for a big feller. There was no point really trying to turn Gary into an Alan Shearer type who could hold the ball up and shield it, instead we had to work on players getting the ball into areas where he wanted it.'

It would be tough for Milne and Lineker as the Foxes struggled on their return to the big time. Leicester lost their opening six matches and the first three at home brought crushing losses: a 4–0 defeat to Notts County and 3–0 to Luton Town and Tottenham Hotspur. The didn't notch until the end of October, against Everton, after eight defeats and two draws. It was the sort of form that Vardy would experience under Nigel Pearson early in the 2014–15 season – and the rescue act, again, would come only as the pressure grew and the season developed.

But Lineker was already starting to hit his rhythm even in that dark opening spell, netting four times before the win over Everton. His twenty-two goals in the league certainly helped the club beat the drop as they finished the season in a respectable fifteenth position out of twenty-two clubs.

And, like Vardy, he would really push on the following season, grabbing his best ever overall total of twenty-nine goals in forty-nine games for the club. That total consisted of twenty-four in the league, three in the FA Cup and two in the League Cup. The only drawback for Leicester was that it now made their main man a target for every club who had ambitions to win the First Division title. After seven seasons of constant progress as a professional footballer, Gary Lineker was about to leave his hometown club, the one where he had spent his whole career. He had finished the campaign as the First Division's joint top scorer, with Chelsea's Kerry Dixon and Everton, the champions, now made their move for Leicester's favourite son.

It was a real blow to the Filbert Street faithful to see their star man leave, but they understood how difficult it was for Lineker to turn down a move to England's then top team. Everton were willing to pay £800,000 for his services; they saw him as a direct and immediate replacement for Andy Gray.

The Merseysiders were the dominant force in English football under Howard Kendall and were denied a domestic and continental treble only by Norman Whiteside's goal for Manchester United in the 1984 FA Cup final. As well as lifting the league title, they had won the European Cup Winners' Cup by beating Rapid Vienna 3–1 in the final. They were top of the tree and many Toffees fans were not at all happy that Lineker was being brought in – not because they didn't like the look of him, but precisely because he was arriving at the expense of their hero, Andy Gray.

The independent Everton website, *ToffeeWeb*, explained it like this: 'On arriving at Goodison Park in July 1985, Gary

Lineker had a similar problem to the one Joe Royle faced at the start of his Everton career, except to a greater extent. The difference lay in the fact that while Royle only replaced fans' favourite Alex Young for one game, Lineker's £850,000 arrival from his home-town club Leicester City led directly to their then idol Andy Gray leaving the club. It was nearly Christmas by the time Lineker won over the Everton crowd – astonishing, given his phenomenal strike-rate of 38 goals on 52 games over the season. But Gray, the talismanic catalyst for the rise to the peak of European football, was a hard act to follow.'

Of course, Vardy has never faced that particular problem. His transfers to the top have been later in life and from the bottom to a struggling Prem team (as the Foxes were when he arrived from Fleetwood). And every team he signed for was glad to see him arrive – and when he exploded into action both fans and management were delighted that they had taken a chance on him. Not so Lineker at Goodison Park. Ironically, and maybe inevitably, given the nature of football, Gary's first game for Everton was at Filbert Street – with the Foxes running out 3–1 winners. Gary remembered it like this: 'At half-time I walked into Leicester's dressing room [by mistake, as he was so used to changing there!]. They hammered us 3–1.'

In a retrospective, the *Leicester Mercury* summed it up as 'an unhappy homecoming', adding, 'It was not often during his career that Gary Lineker was overshadowed at Filbert Street. But that is exactly what happened the last time Leicester City took on Everton on the opening day of the season. On August 17, 1985, Lineker made an immediate return to Filbert Street with his new club after his £800,000 move to Merseyside, but it was not to be a happy homecoming for Leicester's homegrown talent. In fact, it was Lineker's replacement, Mark Bright, who stole the headlines, as he scored twice in a 3–1 victory for City.

'Bobby Smith was also on target that day, while it was Everton defender Derek Mountfield who scored the Toffees' consolation.'

Lineker moved to Goodison for medals and, naturally enough, more money. Not that he would earn anything like Vardy now earns even at England's then top club. In 2011, figures from official PFA union files showed that a top-flight footballer earned around £450 a week – £25,000 a year – while those in the bottom league took home £160 – around £8,500 – in the season that Lineker joined Everton. Obviously he would have earned more at the team that had been top of the league, but even double that would have been only £50k. If he was playing nowadays, Lineker would be on at least £200,000 a week, which is £10 million a year!

I am told by sources that, even before his lucrative new contract of £80,000 a week, Vardy earned around £45,000 a week – almost £2.5 million a year. Okay, this is much less than Lineker would now earn if he were playing in his prime, but proportionately it is certainly a great deal more than Gary got back in the mid-1980s. Lineker did not win any trophies in his time at Everton – he may have had dreams of European glory but, of course, the team were banned from continental competition, as were all English clubs after the tragedy of Heysel in 1985.

Lineker said at the time, 'The final that year was between Barcelona and Steaua Bucharest, and Everton were stronger than both of those teams.'

He also believed that he would have stayed at Goodison for longer than just one season if there had been no European ban – and that he would have enjoyed winning trophies galore. As it was, Everton found it difficult to turn down the offer that came in from Spanish giants Barcelona to buy the player at the end of his debut campaign – especially when Barça offered a more-than-enticing fee of more than £3 million. With revenue lost from no European competition, this money offered a way to replenish the coffers for the club that had always been – and is still – run on sound, tight financial guidelines.

Gary told the football magazine *FourFourTwo* that he accepted that the European ban probably curtailed his Everton career, saying, 'Everton would perhaps have been in a better position to keep me. It was very much Howard [Kendall]'s decision to take the money. When your club tells you they've accepted a bid, you take that as a sign you're not wanted. The opportunity to join a club like Barcelona comes along once in a lifetime, so I had to take it.

'It was a shame, because in an ideal world I'd be able to say, "Give me another couple of years at Everton, let me win a few things, and then I'll go."'

The league season ended bittersweet for Gary as Everton finished runners-up – to bitter local rivals Liverpool. And Liverpool defied them once again in the FA Cup final at Wembley, running out 3–1 winners with a brace from Ian

Rush. Liverpool had secured the league seven days earlier and now notched the double. Gary's consolation was that he scored Everton's goal in the twenty-seventh minute. It put Everton ahead but they could not hold out. Even though they lost, Gary admitted the goal meant a lot to him, saying, 'Scoring in the '86 Cup Final was one of my five most phenomenal moments, the ones you never forget, even though we didn't win.'

The goal came after he fired a shot at Kop keeper Bruce Grobbelaar. The Zimbabwean parried but Lineker, as had happened many times in his career, was alert enough to follow through and hit the ball home. It was a timely goal as England prepared for the 1986 World Cup finals – it wouldn't do his chances of making the team, let alone the squad, any harm, as BBC pundit Jimmy Hill confirmed up in the Wembley press gantry, saying, 'Not a bad goal with the World Cup in mind. If you can catch out your neighbours with a ball like that when they know your play, it might work quite well against the foreigners.'

Lineker's fellow BBC pundit Mark Lawrenson played centre-half against Gary in that final and admitted to the press that they often tease each other about the game. Lawro said, 'That Cup final, of course, with it being against Everton was Gary Lineker's one and only year with Everton. He scored in the first half, [Alan] Hansen's fault – I don't know where he had gone, Hansen, he just completely got caught and he [Lineker] used to give us this great grief about it. But, obviously myself and Hansen used to say to him, "Yeah, but you lost . . . we won."'

That goal and his efforts and overall goals – he netted thirty times in the league, ending the season as top scorer – meant

Gary ultimately never regretted his time on Merseyside. He said he enjoyed playing for the club and the fans came to accept him as he hit the goal trail with a vengeance. Indeed, he talked of having an 'affinity' with them by the end of the season. No doubt Vardy will one day say the same about his experiences at the King Power Stadium – certainly he was the darling of the City fans as the 2015–16 season progressed and he went on that remarkable goalscoring run.

Jamie would love to emulate Gary's success at Leicester and beyond – and no doubt wouldn't even mind playing for Barcelona if Luis Suarez, Lionel Messi or Neymar ever moved on and left an opening! His time at Leicester opened a big world for Lineker as his reputation grew. Like Vardy, he worked hard at his game and was constantly improving. They were similar in that they both accepted the basic premise needed to be a great striker in world football: the more goals you scored the more you would be put on a pedestal.

It was all right people saying that simply scoring did not define you as a centre-forward; that there was much more to it than that; that you could stay in the team if your contribution included assists for others and hard work for the team. But both men realised that that was more often than not the soundbite wheeled out when a striker was going through a barren spell. And, ultimately, if you didn't finally emerge with a hatful of goals, you would be out of the team and replaced by someone who could find the net – regardless of your selfless contribution to the team!

One area where the two men do differ is temperamentally.

Gary is renowned for his calm approach. He was never booked, never mind sent off, in his glittering football career. He was Mr Cool on the pitch – a man who was hot when it came to scoring but who had ice in his veins with his admirable level of self-control. Who can forget the time he pointed to the bench in the World Cup semi-final of 1990 in Italy when Paul Gascoigne lost the plot after getting booked against Germany? The tears started to roll and Lineker beckoned to the England bench that the youngster was in trouble mentally, as he realised that the booking would rule Gascoigne out of the final if England won.

England manager Bobby Robson revealed to the press that he knew Gazza had 'gone' and how 'clever' Lineker had been to alert him of the situation. Robson said, 'I saw his face change, from being aggressive, fighting for the ball, to realising he'd committed an error, and he'd been booked, and he knew now the final was not for him. Tears began to well into his eyes. And Gary Lineker was very clever. He saw it immediately and came as close as he could to me and said, "Watch Gazza. Watch him." He thought now his mind might just go a bit berserk . . .'

Lineker had a clever, quick mind and a fine line in reasoning. He always knew what he wanted and was aware of the world around him. Even in his later career as a TV pundit he managed to continue working for BBC's *Match of the Day* show *and* earn a deal that would see him become presenter of BT's Champions League coverage. He was a top player in football and a top player in life; he knew how to look after himself and early on worked out that the best way to get what you want is to be conciliatory and amenable.

Not for him the rush of blood to the head that often accompanied Jamie Vardy's rise to the top. Vardy himself admitted he could be an irritant and a pain to referee – as we have already touched upon in an earlier chapter. In this sense, he differed dramatically from Lineker, who was very much the 'think first, then act' character, rather than the other way around. Vardy could pick up a yellow card easily, as he was a much more fiery character than Gary. That is not to say that Lineker wasn't determined – I would contend he was (and remains) just as determined and ambitious as the new man who leads the Leicester frontline. It's just a case that both reach their destinations in very different ways, via differing mentalities that are down to their upbringings and outlooks on life.

Gary had a slow-burn, almost leisurely and guaranteed run to the top of English and world football, whereas Jamie, because of his age when he made it in the Prem, is in a rush, and that tends to be reflected in his actions when he's confronted with refereeing decisions and rival players.

I can only think of one incident ever where Gary showed dissent and anger on the football field. That was in the summer of 1992 during England's disastrous campaign in the European Championship finals in Sweden. In what would be England's final match of the campaign – and Lineker's final game for his country – he was subbed by then England boss Graham Taylor.

Clearly discontented at the way the team had played – and that he was seemingly the scapegoat as captain – he threw down the skipper's armband when Taylor took him off. Taylor had appointed Lineker captain when he became boss two years earlier, but the substitution with almost half an hour to go in the game against Sweden would sour their relationship. England failed to win a game and finished bottom of their group. It was a sad way to exit international football for Lineker, who had entertained hopes of surpassing Bobby Charlton's goals record for his country.

I can understand Gary's frustration at the time and I believe it was a general frustration that England were poor and he himself had not lived up to the top billing that would have allowed him to beat Sir Bobby's record that led to the armband controversy. Certainly I don't think for one minute that it was a lack of respect for the armband.

In 2004, Gary backed up the theory that he was dejected about the performances that led to the one rare outburst in his career. He told *The Telegraph*, 'I will always be remembered for throwing down the captain's armband when England manager Graham Taylor substituted me in my final game for my country against Sweden in 1992, but far more disappointing was the fact that I did not taste a single victory from two successive tournaments. In 1992 we were a poor side . . . we went out with a team that had no flair or uniformity. We proved that by drawing 0–0 against both Denmark and France before losing 2–1 to Sweden.'

Final word on 'the armband incident' goes to Stuart Pearce, who would replace Gary as skipper. In his autobiography, *Psycho*, he recalls that the mood before the Sweden match was optimistic and that the team were relaxed after going to see Bruce Springsteen in concert! That in itself surprises me, as Pearce is more renowned as an aficionado of punk rather than the blue-collar rock Bruce is known for, but even more surprising is that old Psycho seemed to back Taylor rather than Lineker over the incident. In the book he says, 'I am sure Graham would not have pulled Gary off unless he thought he could win the match by doing it . . . Gary was clearly annoyed and made it look bad by taking off his armband and throwing it on to the floor, in my direction, as I was taking over the captaincy.'

Pearce's opinion surprises me, as surely England would have been better placed to score with the man who had already hit forty-eight goals for his country playing until the final minute. And couldn't Taylor have brought Smith on to partner Lineker, rather than replacing him?

I would think that, if it had been Vardy in the same position, there would have been a much more stringent reaction than a simple throwing down of an armband! Taylor would probably have got the band thrown at him, along with a right mouthful!

Lineker's fine season with the Toffees meant he did become one of the first names in the England squad for the 1986 World Cup in Mexico. I should mention that he never got booked playing for England, either, although he never failed to put in a proper shift, as his goals tally would confirm. Like Vardy's, his debut for his country came when he was at Leicester. Gary walked on proudly to face the 'auld enemy' Scotland on 26 May 1984, aged twenty-three. Jamie's debut, as we have mentioned, would come much later in his life – when he was twenty-eight, to be precise. Gary came on as a sub after seventy-two minutes, replacing Tony Woodcock up front in a home international championship match at Hampden Park, Glasgow.

It would be a disappointment when Gary was not chosen for that summer's tour of South America – that was when John Barnes truly came of age as an England player when he 'did a Brazil' by scoring against them by dribbling through their defence as if they were ghosts. But Gary would be back the following March when he duly scored his first goal for his country.

It came against the Republic of Ireland the following March. Starting with the number 10 on his back and partnering Mark Hateley, Gary scored England's winner in a 2–1 victory in a friendly at Wembley. Gary was 'well chuffed' to have grabbed the goal that separated the two teams. Trevor Steven also scored his first international goal, while there were debuts for Tottenham's Chris Waddle, Manchester United keeper Gary Bailey and, also as a sub, Nottingham Forest striker Peter Davenport. Former Arsenal hero Liam Brady, by then at Inter Milan, scored a consolation for the visitors.

The England team that day read: Gary Bailey, Viv Anderson, Kenny Sansom, Terry Butcher, Mark Wright, Chris Waddle, Bryan Robson, Ray Wilkins, Trevor Steven, Mark Hateley and Lineker. It was a momentous day for the Leicester boy, as not only did he score but his display convinced national boss Bobby Robson that he should now be a cornerstone of his team. Lineker now stayed in the side as England's number-one striker until the fallout with Graham Taylor six years later. During the summer of 1985 Gary grabbed a brace in England's 5–0 victory over the United States in Los Angeles, and was regularly finding the net for his country in the remaining World Cup qualifiers – although he had now left the Foxes for Everton.

Gary went on to score five hat-tricks for England and is currently their third-highest top scorer after Rooney and Charlton. Obviously, Vardy will never get anywhere near that record, being such a late bloomer in the Premier League, let alone on the international front. But Jamie has told pals he is determined to do his best to leave his mark on the England front and he is the first to admit he is in Lineker's slipstream, and that Gary remains not only one of the all-time greats of Leicester, but also of England.

In the 2015–16 season Vardy certainly made inroads into Lineker's legend at Leicester as he went on that incredible scoring spree. Another Foxes hero, Alan Birchenall, agreed that Vardy has the makings of another Lineker. He told the *Leicester Mercury* in November 2015, 'During my time at the club, I have seen only one other player progress as quickly as Jamie, from a slow start to getting where he is today, closing in on Ruud van Nistelrooy's Premier League record. The other one who falls into that category was when I first saw Gary Lineker. His first half-dozen games were not the best and Gary would admit that. I never thought he would go on to achieve what he did in his career. The same with Vards. He was a rough diamond when he first came in and struggled in his first season, but to see how he is playing now is unbelievable. It is credit to the lad for the attitude he has shown.'

After the Foxes won 2–1 at Norwich in October 2015, boss Claudio Ranieri said it's 'good for us if he is being compared [to

Lineker]. I'm happy about that.' But City's big central defender Robert Huth highlighted the central difference between Gary and Jamie – how Jamie has a more aggressive temperament. Huth told the press, 'He's just really, really annoying. He never gives up, he's always on your case. The amount of balls he got today when he was second favourite to win it but managed to get a foot on it, get the free-kick or throw-in 60–70 yards up the pitch, and take the pressure off us. We love Jamie here. I try to be on his side in training, it makes it a much easier session.'

And Huth's centre-back partner Wes Morgan confirmed that essential difference of character, saying, 'He's showing what he can do on the big stage. He's a pain in the backside for any defender. He's a soldier, he keeps going for ninety minutes and never seems to get tired.'

But there is one area in which Vardy and Lineker are interminably joined: they have both had a packet of crisps named in their honour! Gary, of course, has been the TV face of Walkers Crisps for many years in a variety of entertaining adverts. And, towards the end of 2015, Walkers also paid tribute to Jamie by producing 32,000 packets of specially branded, ready-salted-flavour crisps to hand to fans arriving for Leicester's home match against Chelsea. 'Vardy Salted' crisps were made as a special souvenir to celebrate his setting that new Premier League record of scoring in eleven successive games. Walkers, based in Leicester, had previously paid tribute to Lineker with 'Salt & Lineker' crisps – and now Jamie had got in on the act. A spokesman for Walkers said, 'We are excited to announce that we have created limited edition packs of "Vardy Salted" crisps to celebrate Jamie Vardy's record-breaking goals in eleven straight games and following incredible social media public demand. Packs of ready-salted-flavour crisps with a celebratory image of Vardy and in the colour of Leicester's Blue will be handed out exclusively to fans at the Leicester City versus Chelsea game.'

That's Vardy and Lineker for you. Two Leicester legends from different eras, both with chips on their shoulders – and both proud of it and of their colourful Foxes heritage. Gary would now watch on in amazement and tweet his encouragement from afar as Jamie embarked on that record-breaking goal run.

CHAPTER EIGHT

RUUD AWAKENING

Who'd have ever thought it? That the boy from non-league would one day match one of the world's greatest strikers by scoring in ten consecutive Premier League games – and then break his record in the very next? When Jamie Vardy equalled Ruud van Nistelrooy's achievement by scoring at Newcastle on 21 November 2015, his fairy-tale rise from nowhere to the very top of the footballing world was complete. The Premier League's late bloomer had gone and done it – and made headlines on the back pages and the sports shows around the world. From non-league to global star, the transformation was remarkable. It was a later wonder that there was now talk of a Hollywood movie to document the achievement – indeed, many pundits in Fleet Street contended that, if it had been mooted as a film *before* Vardy's goals feast, you would have dismissed the idea as poppycock. You'd have said it was just too unbelievable – that cinema audiences would have stayed away. Because it would have been seen as just a stretch of the imagination too far.

Yet a motion picture at St James' Park, Newcastle, that bright November afternoon it wasn't – it was reality. As was the moment when Jamie would surpass Ruud's ten goals on the trot in the next game at the King Power, against Manchester United. With that eleventh goal, it was as if the gods of fate were smiling on Jamie – not only had he beaten Ruud, he had done it against the team with whom the Dutchman had achieved his own brilliant record. Yes, it was deeply ironic that Vardy claimed the record while playing against the Reds.

But it also highlighted just how good Vardy's run was: he had achieved it in the colours of Leicester, who in the previous season had been battling relegation, while Van Nistelrooy had made his goalscoring exploits for United, who were regular Premier League title winners and Champions League contenders. It was more difficult for Jamie, as he did not have the slick, world-class talents around him that Ruud could rely on to grab his goals haul. He had to carve out many of his own openings and speed through for his own goals, while Ruud had it much easier with the likes of David Beckham supplying a steady stream of pinpoint crosses and assists, some of which even *I* could probably have converted!

That is in no way meant to be a slight on the Leicester class of 2015. They too had players who were making a name for themselves and who would not have looked out of place at Old Trafford. Riyad Mahrez, for example, was already the subject of coveted glances from Europe's giants, including United themselves, who felt he could do a job in the traditions of Ryan Giggs. But the point here is that lucky old Ruud already *had* Giggs crossing to him in the box – along with Beckham and Paul Scholes! So for me Vardy's matching of Ruud was a much greater achievement, and, when he surpassed him, well, it was extraordinary, an out-of-this-world feat that may never be equalled in the Premier League.

The goal that would equal the Dutchman's record came near half-time when Jamie was played through by Leonardo Ulloa. He still had work to do but his pace took him clear and he coolly slotted the ball home past hapless keeper Rob Elliot. It was a fine finish, especially taking into account the fact that Vardy had been a major doubt to start, after suffering a hip injury while away on international duty with England – an injury that had cost him two starts for the national team.

The bookies were well aware that Vardy was on course to equal the record – and that he could still match it against Man United if he had been ruled out of the Newcastle match. And bookies BetVictor also made the pertinent point that, if Jamie did match Ruud, his feat would also be more accomplished as he would have done it in one season, while Ruud's had been achieved over two. BetVictor explained the whole situation before the game at St James', telling Fleet Street sports desks, 'Leicester City striker Jamie Vardy is a huge doubt for Saturday's clash with Newcastle as he looks to match Ruud van Nistelrooy's Premier League goalscoring record. Vardy is looking to equal former Man Utd striker Van Nistelrooy's feat of scoring in 10 consecutive Premier League games and he may have a pain-killing injection in his hip so he can feature at St James' Park.

'The England man, who missed the two recent international friendlies, picked up the problem after scoring in Leicester's recent win over Watford and the 28-year-old is contemplating having some pain relief so he can take his place against the Magpies rather than face the prospect of scoring against Manchester United the following week. The former Fleetwood man's record is arguably more impressive than Van Nistelrooy's because the Dutch legend's goal streak was split across the 2002/03 and 2003/04 seasons and a time period of six months as opposed to Vardy's four months.

'Vardy is a 23/20 shot with BetVictor to score on Tyneside, but if he is ruled out through injury the striker will still be able to equal the record, albeit against tougher opposition next week when the Foxes face United.'

In the event, Vardy scored in *both* games, equalling the record at Newcastle and then obliterating it at home to Man United the following week.

After Leicester's 3–0 win at St James', Jamie paid tribute to the backroom staff who had ensured he would be on the pitch to have a go at equalling Ruud's feat. Jamie said, 'The physios have done brilliantly to get me fit. We know we can cause teams problems and are solid at the back too. We have a never-say-die attitude and will fight for each other until the end.'

Foxes boss Claudio Ranieri paid tribute to his star man, who was also named Man of the Match at Newcastle. The Italian admitted that he almost had to leave Vardy out of his team because of those injury concerns, and pinpointed just why he is such a dangerous striker when he is on the top of his game, telling a press briefing, 'He was very, very close. I spoke with all our medical staff and at the end. They told me that he was okay and that was good for us. Jamie is an easy boy. He doesn't think about the expectation. He wants to win and show his best performance. He is a worker for the team. I love him.

'He's not a striker who waits for the ball and then scores a goal. He works very hard for the team and then scores a goal. For all the strikers it's very important to continue to score. That's Jamie and also [Shinji] Okazaki and Leo [Ulloa]. Leo was our top goal scorer last season and he continues to work hard, even when he hasn't scored and hasn't played.

'That is the right way. I need twenty-five players who believe something is good for the team, not selfish. They are involved in this project. I also want to say also thank you to our fans. They travelled for four hours and I want to say thank you to everybody.'

Ranieri then elaborated a little more on Vardy's standing among strikers on a worldwide scale, and compared him to one of the game's best ever players, stating, 'It is fantastic for Jamie Vardy. He is a great champion and did well in training. I am glad because we played like a team. I also had Gabriel Batistuta at Fiorentina score in eleven consecutive matches and I hope Jamie can achieve this.' That was some tribute from a manager who had worked across the globe – Jamie was especially 'thrilled' that Ranieri compared him to the legendary Batistuta. The Argentine centre-forward is one of the greatest strikers *ever* to grace the game and many pundits, including myself, would argue he was even better than Van Nistelrooy.

In a nice touch, Newcastle fans joined their Leicester counterparts in applauding Vardy as he left the pitch with about fifteen minutes to go. Ranieri wanted to protect Jamie because of his injury problem and so hauled him off early. He earned rapturous applause from both sets of supporters, who had been aware he could equal the record by scoring. Newcastle fans may have been hurting badly at their own team's obvious inadequacies but they proved they are magnanimous and true lovers of the game by standing up out of their seats and putting their hands together. A fantastic gesture from a fantastic, loyal set of fans who stand by their team through thick and thin and are big enough to appreciate the feats of rivals.

Fans from other clubs – and Leicester, of course – bombarded Twitter with a series of messages to congratulate Jamie. Will Ridgard led the way with the 'Vardy having a party' line: 'Jamie Vardy's having a party. Absolutely superb achievement. Remember that he's from non-league!' Malik Aden tweeted, 'Jamie Vardy has now scored in ten consecutive Premier League games, equalling Ruud van Nistelrooy's record from 2003. WOW.' Ben Phipps said, 'Vardy is an absolute machine! Congrats man!' Jack Winter added, 'It's happening: Jamie Vardy is indeed having a party.' Twitter user 'Magnum' made the point that Jamie had come a long way in a short time after finally making the big league, going on to say, 'Can't believe how far Jamie Vardy has come. That's mad like.' Leicester City fan Lewis Edwards tweeted his warm congratulations to his hero: 'Huge congratulations to Jamie Vardy. Unreal.' And another Twitter user applauded Jamie but also added a few words of caution: 'Vardy is a king man, let's just hope he isn't a one season wonder.'

Before the Newcastle game, Van Nistelrooy himself took to Instagram to say he hoped Vardy would score and equal his record and then go on to surpass it. Ruud said, 'Records are there to be broken. Go on Vardy7, all the best and good luck!' That was a nice touch by Ruud and I was told by sources in Holland that he was 'delighted' when Vardy equalled his feat and 'very pleased for Jamie' when he finally ended Ruud's record run. The Dutchman would make public his joy for Vardy after the Leicester striker broke his record, tweeting, 'Well done Vardy7! You're number one now and you deserved it!' To which Jamie replied, 'Thank you! Means a lot!'

In between the Newcastle and Man United games, Van Nistelrooy had once again spoken about how he hoped Jamie would keep cool and beat his record. He made his views clear when he spoke at the Oxford Union on the Tuesday, sandwiched in between the two games. He was asked what it would mean to him personally if Vardy snatched his record and Ruud said he was absolutely fine with the prospect, elaborating to say, 'I sent him a message of support last weekend on social media and I really meant it. It would be fantastic for him. I really mean it, records are there to be broken. He can score one on Saturday, in fact I hope he does but hopefully United score three and win 3–1. But no, seriously, if he does it, I'll be delighted for him.'

Vardy had made it clear that if he did make the history books it wouldn't just be down to his predatory skills – he wanted his teammates to take equal billing for the work they had put into provide him with the opportunities he so brilliantly devoured. Before the match against United he told Sky Sports News HQ, 'It's about hard work and the players that I've got around me getting me into positions where I'm able to put the ball in the back of the net; it's as simple as that. It's a joy to play in that team. In our first year in the Premier League we didn't know what to expect. It was quicker and more physical. Confidence is sky high but everyone is very grounded. Having experience of that really does help you, and if we carry on this way then who knows what will happen?'

He admitted the goals run had taken him by surprise – that he never anticipated it and that he had not even set himself a goals target for the season, something that many top strikers do at the start of each campaign in August. His aim was simply to do his best for the club and see where that took him and the team.

Former Sky Sports pundit-turned-Valencia boss Gary Neville added his congratulations to Jamie's achievements, while admitting he was as surprised as the player that it had come to pass, given how Jamie had initially struggled to find his feet in the top flight. Gary said, 'It's been an incredible rise from non-league football right through to the Premier League, but the biggest jump in some ways has been the meteoric rise in the last twelve months.

'You've got to remember he only scored twenty goals in sixty-three appearances in the Championship, so you weren't expecting it at the start of last season – for a striker to come into the Premier League and do what he's done.'

Gary pointed out that Jamie had upped his game dramatically – whereas he had previously sometimes grabbed at chances, he now was cool and deadly. He had become a different player; a killer hitman.

BBC Sport made the point that it wasn't just Jamie who was breaking goal records in 2015 – one striker in Spain and one in Germany were making headlines. And both were the sorts of world-class players Vardy would love to be compared to when it comes to goal scoring. The programme spokesman went on, 'Cristiano Ronaldo became Real Madrid's all-time leading scorer with a goal against Levante on 17 October, moving him ahead of Raul's tally of 323. He has since added two more goals to his tally. Bayern Munich's Robert Lewandowski, meanwhile, has enjoyed a purple patch most strikers can only dream of. This season the Poland striker became the fastest foreign player to one hundred goals in the Bundesliga, and boasts an impressive twenty-five goals in twenty-two appearances for club and country.'

They were remarkable achievements by two of the greatest attacking players of the modern era – and Jamie's was worthy of the same mention in that his consecutive goals feat came in the Premier League, which is arguably much harder to score regularly in than La Liga or the Bundesliga.

Vardy broke Van Nistelrooy's twelve-year record at the King Power Stadium on 28 November against Man United, as the clubs fought out an entertaining 1–1 draw. Honours may have been even between the teams but, as at Newcastle, the day belonged to Jamie. He smashed his way into football's history books by scoring that record-breaking eleventh goal on the trot when he outpaced Man United's leaden backline on the twenty-five-minute mark. Naturally, he celebrated wildly, with a few choice swear words in there for good measure! Jamie appeared to shout, 'It's me, me, me, fucking me!' Later he told reporters, 'It's unbelievable. I think I got a bit carried away with myself in the celebration. I don't think I can repeat what I said, to be honest! Yeah, I'm obviously delighted. It's incredible.'

And then he added, 'There was relief. But I wasn't going to let it get to me. I wasn't going to let it affect my performance. The record was not in my mind, it would have affected my performance and the team's, and that's the last thing I wanted to do. I can think about it when I'm home but as soon as I cross the white line all I should be concentrating on is my football. That's what I've been doing and exactly what I will continue to do.

'I just kept my head down and concentrated. The main thing was the performance. We all put in a very good shift today and a point was probably a fair result. When I got back into the dressing room, the reaction from the lads was brilliant. They gave me a round of applause. The gaffer came in and said a few words and he's left a shirt that he's signed.'

Ranieri was equally delighted for his player, telling reporters, 'It's an incredible achievement for Jamie and fantastic for football . . . We had two objectives: to win the match and try to help Vardy break the record. Jamie made the record; it's fantastic for us. Five years ago he played in non-league. It's difficult to grow up so quickly, and this fantastic man is not only our goalscorer but he presses, he works hard, he is important.

'I signed his shirt and I dated it, because my signature is important. I wrote "Great achievement, great record, 11 goals in a row" – also his teammates signed it. We drew the match and the performance was good and I am very happy with the record. I hope this record keeps on for a long time and we are very proud about it. All his teammates helped him to achieve it.'

Ranieri was also interested in United star Bastian Schweinsteiger's claim that Vardy was similar to Germany's record goalscorer Miroslav Klose. He added, 'I heard Schweinsteiger say Vardy is like Klose for their national team. Yes, because he is important for us like Klose is for the national team.'

Even Man United boss Louis van Gaal wanted to add his congratulations. He said, 'The goal he scored is amazing because it is not so easy. I can say our organisation is bad but he is provoking that also. It is a fantastic record to have, eleven matches in a row. Not many players will do that.'

And other pros and pundits were keen to add their praise for the achievement. Former Stoke defender Danny Higginbotham, now a respected tactical commentator for *The Independent*, tweeted, 'Vardy outstanding and deserves it. LCFC love to counter attack and MUFC fell into the trap just like many teams before.'

And Gary Lineker tweeted, 'Vardy! He scores when he wants.'

Goalkeeper Carlo Cudicini added, 'Vardy . . . what a story!

Congratulations for the new record.' Higginbotham also made some incisive comments about how and when Vardy is most likely to punish teams. He wrote in *The Independent*, 'Vardy has scored on nine of the thirteen occasions when he has been Ranieri's furthest forward player. He is particularly dangerous in the second half when the opposition become more vulnerable, lured by Leicester's deep-lying defensive line into playing a very high line . . . Nine of Vardy's thirteen goals have come in the second half. When Leicester turn over possession, he and others head into the space the full-backs have vacated and . . . the blue-shirted player in possession will hit that area. That in turn drags the opposition centre-back into a full-back area he doesn't want to be in.'

Leicester teammates also chipped in on Twitter. Jeff Schlupp tweeted, 'He's done it!! Congrats @vardy7 on breaking the record! #11inarow.' Andy King added, '@vardy7 what an achievement that cheer when his goal was announced was the loudest I've heard down the KP.'

Fans throughout the game also piped up with their tributes. 'John' said, 'Well done Vardy. I love to see any player, or any team achieve something like that. To score twelve goals and break a record is something remarkable.' And 'Steven' also chipped in with praise, all the more worthy as he was a lifelong Manchester United fan! He said, 'Vardy is just amazing. I wish we had him at Old Trafford – he's so fast, lean and a natural goalscorer, just what we need at the moment. He must be the best buy for £1 million since the time we bought Eric Cantona from Leeds for that amount.

And I reckon he could have a similar immediate impact for us if we could get him, but he'd probably cost us £20 million now he's broken Ruud's record!'

Another football fan added a touch of humour to the proceedings, imagining how Louis van Gaal might deal with Vardy if he signed him! He said, 'I really hope he stays at Leicester. Could you imagine the conversation if he went to Utd? Vardy: "Hi boss, can't believe I'm now following in Van Nistelrooy's footsteps and I can't wait to start banging in the goals for you." Van Gaal: "Calm down lad, that was in the old days. There will be no attacking or trying to score on my watch . . . is that clear? Rooney will show you how we do it."'

The goal against United broke another record, as well as Ruud's. It was Jamie's fourteenth goal of the campaign so far and meant he had set a new Leicester City record for goals scored in a Premier League season, overhauling the thirteen netted by Tony Cottee in the 1999–2000 season. And we were only at the end of November! There were still six months of the season to come.

Vardy was on fire and City fans were dreaming that he might even double his tally by May 2016.

There was much optimism that he could now surpass the all-time record of consecutive goals recorded in the top flight. To do that, he would need to score in his next two games after the United match. That record had been achieved way back in the 1931–2 season when Sheffield United's Jimmy Dunne scored in twelve consecutive matches – with a tally of eighteen. The Dubliner was a true hotshot but Leicester fans will be hoping Vardy does not suffer the same fate that befell Dunne after his record-breaker. As broadcaster RTÉ Sport in Ireland pointed out, one minute he was king of the block, the next he was yesterday's man, continuing to say, '[He] set the record for scoring in consecutive games when he scored eighteen in twelve games between 21 October 1931 and 1 January 1932. That record still stands. His goalscoring exploits soon attracted the attention of Arsenal and Dunne went on to play four seasons in London with the Gunners . . . the period of success at Arsenal was brief, however. In the years to come, Dunne would be eclipsed at the club by the arrival of legendary striker Ted Drake . . . Dunne would only make two appearances in the following two seasons. By 1936 his time in the English top flight was at an end.'

That could be seen as a salutary tale for Jamie if he considered upping sticks from Leicester for a so-called 'Big Four' team. The big shot at Sheffield United found the going much tougher at Arsenal.

Back in 2015, overhauling Dunne's achievement would prove a record too far for Vardy. Even though Leicester beat Swansea in their next outing, he was unable to find the net, which meant he did not equal Dunne's record, never mind surpass it. Not that Jamie minded: as he always maintained, what mattered was the team, not the individual. He would stress he was a team player; that the result counted, not his breaking records, although clearly he was delighted if that was a consequence of his own efforts.

We've examined how he equalled the record and then went on to break it, but in the next chapter let's have a closer look at the goals that led up to those remarkable achievements: the nine that provided the backbone for his place in history.

CHAPTER NINE

THE RECORD BREAKER

It all began innocuously enough. At the start of the 2015–16 season few would have predicted he would be among the Premier League's top scorers, let alone tear up a page in the record books by destroying Ruud van Nistelrooy's twelve-year-old achievement. Sure, there were signs that Jamie was in better shape than in the previous campaign, when he had scored just five Premier League goals in thirty-seven appearances. He had actually amassed more yellow cards – six – than goals back then. By August 2015, he had clearly more chance of grabbing more than five goals in the forthcoming season. He looked fitter, he looked sharper and he looked 'up for it'. He also had the advantage of knowing that those alongside him were in the same position: they had, after all, battled together at the end of the previous campaign to avoid what had once looked like inevitable relegation. Yet, still, I don't know anyone on the sports desks of Fleet Street who was saying that Jamie Vardy was going to shock us all by becoming the top No. 9 in England over the next few months.

It seemed all the more unlikely when you also took into account the fact that the man who engineered that remarkable retreat from the drop zone, namely Nigel Pearson, had now left the club. Passionate, no-nonsense Nige had gone and been replaced by a man many in Fleet Street – and, let's be honest here – among the fans who packed out the King Power week in, week out, believed would prove to be a disastrous choice. On the face of it Claudio Ranieri, often portrayed as a bumbling Italian (even by himself), did not appear to be someone who could take the club onwards and upwards. In his last place of work, he had failed as manager of the Greek national team and now he was being asked to build on Pearson's work at Leicester. Not for nothing had Ranieri become known as the 'Tinkerman' in his time as boss of Chelsea earlier in his career. He liked to rotate his team selections but, if he did that at the King Power, would City – and Vardy – now lose the impetus they had picked up in the last days of Pearson's reign?

All that hard graft would be for nothing – and Jamie and co. would most likely be fighting another relegation battle.

But it didn't work out like that. In fact, as far as Vardy was concerned, it couldn't really have worked out much better. Far from tinkering, Ranieri did, of course, stick with Pearson's work and told his first-team squad he was going to stand by them and keep the same team as far as was possible, match by match. That was a tremendous boost to the players, who now felt secure and able to express themselves without fear of being rested or dropped on the whims of a tinkering manager. It was as if Ranieri had learned from his time at Chelsea, and while in charge of Greece, that you played your best men when they were all available – and you left well alone if you stumbled on a project that had experienced success.

That was music to Vardy's ears. Ranieri had told him he believed in him and that he also believed he could be a great goalscorer, and now he would have the chance to prove it, backed up by the same teammates who had ended the season together. He knew that, in the likes of Riyad Mahrez and Marc Albrighton, he was working with players who were on the same wavelength as he was, who would provide the assists and crosses he could thrive upon. It was a great boost to personal and team morale that Ranieri basically let them get on with it, supplying his own inimitable brand of support and management, as the season got under way on 8 August 2015.

How big a boost they'd received could be garnered from how Vardy and his teammates performed in their opening match. They beat Sunderland 4–2 at home and Jamie grabbed the first goal on eleven minutes with a fine header. City were actually 3–0 up within half an hour as they emerged from the traps like greyhounds. It was a great start to the season for Vardy and Leicester – the Premier League table after Week One showed them standing proudly at the top, and this just months after they had struggled to survive relegation.

Vardy told pals of his delight at scoring with his head

and Ranieri praised him and his fellow scorers. Ranieri told reporters, 'It was a very good start and I am very happy with my players in the first match, which is so important in front of our fans. I told my players to be the warriors for them. The performance was outstanding from the beginning. The whole team played well.'

However you would still have been hard pushed to find anyone who would have predicted Vardy's scoring feats – if anything, most pundits were purring more about the display of Vardy's partner-in-crime, Mahrez, who netted twice against the Black Cats. He was voted Man of the Match and was generally viewed as the player who would press on most during the season and become a magnet for the so-called 'Big Four' teams. If he continued his form, they would surely be circling like vultures for his signature when the winter transfer window opened the following January.

Mahrez was the one who was making the headlines after that opener. He would continue to do so with brilliant performances as the season moved from summer to autumn to winter, but he would eventually be eclipsed by Vardy, as it became clear the former non-league man was going to challenge Van Nistelrooy's record. After the Sunderland match, Jamie was more than happy to share the limelight – as indeed he was during his record run – and still no one foresaw how he would shape the next few months in his own image. Or how that remarkable run would even have Hollywood considering making a movie about him – recreating how a lowly footballer had hit the peak of the game. Truly, this was a fairy tale with few equals in sporting history – and if it happened it could possibly be a bestselling biopic. Certainly, Foxes fans would rush out to buy it when it finally came out on DVD!

The team now kicked on, winning at West Ham and drawing with Spurs. Jamie was playing well and contributing to the team's early unbeaten run. But there was still no suggestion or inkling that he was about to go on that record-breaking goals run. He had scored one goal in three games and had, in many pundits' minds, been overshadowed by the skills of Mahrez, who had scored four goals in the first three games.

But that was all about to change – and change big time.

It began at the unlikeliest of places: Dean Court, Bournemouth. The Cherries had been promoted from the Championship only the previous season and were odds-on to go straight back then. But, under the astute guidance of boss Eddie Howe, they were playing good football and proving they were worth at least a chance in the Premier League. And it was here at Dean Court that Vardy stepped up to the plate and gave a massive hint of what he was all about when he rescued Leicester's unbeaten start to the season by scoring a late penalty to make it 1–1.

Vardy showed he had nerves of steel to match his goal prowess with that spot-kick, as no other City player had the mettle or inclination to take it. Jamie would tell *The Sun* later, 'There weren't many putting their name forward for the penalty and they were pointing at me. So I stepped up and lashed it as hard as I could and luckily it went in. We ground out a draw, which was probably a fair result, and with the international break coming it just keeps the momentum going.'

The *Daily Mail* described the goal in this way, highlighting how Vardy won it and despatched it: 'Leicester's pressure reached a crescendo when, with four minutes remaining, Vardy – terrier-like in his running all match – burst past two players and into the box where he was chopped down by the sliding Steve Cook. He stepped up to thunder the penalty in.' Terrier-like – a fine description of Jamie the pest, always nipping at the heels of defenders and never letting go until he hurt them with his goals.

Ranieri praised his man for keeping his nerve and for the fact that he had kept the unbeaten run alive. It extended their unbeaten away record to five games – a club record in the Premier League. Ranieri said, 'I am very pleased with the point. Bournemouth are very well organised and I told their manager they're fantastic and play like an orchestra. They make a fantastic goal but we showed very good character in the second half and deserved our goal.'

Leicester were unbeaten and third in the Premier League and Jamie was celebrating his goal at Bournemouth with the news that he had also been called up for the England squad. It would be a fortnight before he got the chance to grab his second consecutive Premier League goal in what would become known as the record run. And, after the exertions of recent weeks, he and City were content to see that it was relegation favourites and fellow Midlanders Aston Villa who were due at the King Power Stadium on Sunday, 13 September. That said, Villa put up a spirited display, losing only 3–2, and that after taking a 2–0 lead.

THE RECORD BREAKER

My spies at the King Power suggested the Foxes had taken the game too easy, maybe assuming that Villa – after the summer departures of Fabian Delph, Ron Vlaar and Christian Benteke – would be easy pickings. But under their then boss Tim Sherwood they battled hard, and it was only Leicester's own growing determination and eye for goals that helped them get back into a match they looked to have lost.

Leicester did well: they came away with a creditable 2–2 draw when many left empty-handed. Ritchie De Laet pulled one back with a header and that man Vardy made it 2–2 with a poacher's finish before Nathan Dyer's header won it for the Foxes. The win moved them up to second in the table behind Manchester City, but again there was no talk about Vardy's goal exploits, even though he had two in two. No, the conversations again reverted to the brilliance of Riyad Mahrez, and how he had inspired the team to an incredible comeback.

That did not worry Jamie. He remained calm and determined to be a team player. He did not want individual glory: he wanted more than anything to be in a successful team. He had no thoughts of any records at this stage, of course – he was only two games down the road towards the Van Nistelrooy record and he would have to do it the hard way if he were to make it three goals in three matches.

They don't come much harder than playing Stoke City away. Renowned as a team who play hard and are roared on by their crowd, few visitors relish playing at the Britannia. It is no place for faint hearts and, as Vardy will testify, it's a destination where you certainly know you have been in a game at the end of ninety minutes.

Yet again, Leicester showed real guts to come back for a point. Yet again, the Foxes fell two goals down. And, yet again, their resilience would save the day. Once more, Mahrez was the inspiration, this time scoring from the penalty spot and then setting up Vardy for the equaliser. But suddenly, even though Mahrez had inspired, it was Jamie who took the main headlines. BBC Sport declared him to be the Man of the Match, pointing out, 'Leicester striker Jamie Vardy has scored in three successive Premier League games for the first time and threatened to win the game for his side after his equaliser.'

Vardy was starting to take the spotlight, buoyed by his England call-up and feeling at home in the Leicester side as a regular and starting to score regularly. He was gradually becoming a key man for club and country. Foxes boss Ranieri again praised him and Mahrez, but cautioned about getting carried away by results, especially as the backline was proving so leaky. He said, 'Winning from 2–0 down is not possible every time. In the second half we reacted very well. But we need to concentrate better so we don't concede so often.'

The fans were also starting to take note of Vardy's goals and work ethic. Dejan said, 'People only talk about Mahrez, who's amazing, but what about Vardy? He's quick, great finishing, and his fighting spirit is awesome.' And John Kirk added, 'I keep reading about Mahrez being the man who's driving City on, but what about Vardy's contributions? He cannot stop scoring now and is turning out to be a gem for Leicester. What a buy for a million quid – and from non-league, too! Give me Vardy over the likes of Rooney any day.'

At the end of September 2015 Jamie would make it four games on the run that he had scored in – he would actually grab a brace – but it would also be the game when the doom merchants claimed Leicester had been found out as they crashed 5–2 at home to Arsenal. They would be proved wrong.

Although it finished 5–2, some pundits changed the score to Vardy 2, Sanchez 3, in tribute to the two great strikers, with Alexis Sanchez's hat-trick proving the difference between the teams. It ended Leicester's unbeaten start to the season but it had been Vardy first on the scoresheet with a fine finish to put Leicester 1–0 ahead after thirteen minutes. Jamie netted for the second time almost on the ninety minutes when he hammered the ball home, only for the Gunners to demand the last word with their fifth goal, this time Olivier Giroud scoring from a cross.

On paper it looked like a hammering and it was clear that Ranieri would need to look into his Italian notebook on defending, his nation being after all the masters of the art. Otherwise the exploits of Vardy and Mahrez would count for nothing if they kept being outscored at the other end of the pitch. Ranieri admitted as much, saying that Vardy's goals had been the only highlight of a disappointing day, and that, 'It was difficult at the beginning and difficult at the end. We touched the post twice and that was our best moment. Arsenal are dangerous on the counter attack. The first half was good and open but at 3–1 it was difficult. We shoot at goal a lot of times but Petr Cech is Petr Cech. I hope if we could hold at 2–1 we could force it until late in the game, but Alexis Sanchez scored early. The second half was then finished. We must begin again now and repeat this start to the season. We must show character in the next match.'

Even so, City remained in the title race and Jamie had now scored in four successive games. His bandwagon towards the record was gaining momentum with every match. He was on a wonder run; put simply, Vardy just could not stop scoring goals. He had the Midas touch.

They say a week is a long time in football, but for Vardy and co. it was just long enough for them to get the Arsenal loss out of their systems – and for them to get back on track at Norwich. This would be the fifth game on the trot that he scored in for the Foxes, and he would contribute to a 2–1 victory. And, by now, people were starting to sit up and take notice: they were starting to realise that the boy was not only something special, but that he was onto something special, too. Vardy was suddenly becoming headline news: a new scoring sensation in English football and a great hope for the underdogs of the Premier League and, ultimately, the England national team.

Vardy put City 1–0 up at Carrow Road just before the half-hour mark as he converted from the penalty spot after he was fouled by Sebastien Bassong. Jamie had raced on to a pass from N'Golo Kanté and, as would be the case in many matches that season, he was just too fast for the big defender, leaving Bassong with little choice but to commit a professional foul or see Vardy score without the need for a penalty. Jamie said he was pleased with his goal and that he was enjoying his run of conversions, but added, as always, that the fact the team triumphed was more important than personal glory.

It was a theme Ranieri also spoke of after the game. He was delighted for Vardy – and delighted *with* him for his battling qualities as well as the goal glut – but he also stressed it was the teamwork that was key. It was fighting and winning, or losing, as a team that would bring rewards at the end of the season. It was the idea that if the team were doing well, then individuals would inevitably also be doing well.

Ranieri told reporters, 'For me, it's important to maintain the English spirit in the team. We have very good English players, but also the others. Today was a battle. We knew that after our defeat against Arsenal we wanted a good performance and I'm satisfied – I like it when there is a battle. The second goal was fantastic because we knew Norwich were pushing hard and were very strong, so it was important to score again. But we created eight or nine chances and it was a good match for the fans.'

Of Vardy individually, he added, 'It's not only scoring goals, it's important how he is pressing. That helps the players behind him. He's in a great moment. Strikers live for this. His performance was important.'

Sky Sports' pundit Phil Thompson, the ex-Liverpool and England defender, has as good an eye as anyone to assess the ability of a striker – after all, he played against some of the best in his heyday. So it was interesting to hear him cheerleading for Vardy to be given a proper chance in an England shirt after the Norwich match. He said of Vardy, who was also selected as the

Man of the Match, 'Vardy is on fire at the moment, and should be given a chance for England in the next couple of weeks. [Jeffrey] Schlupp added the pace that Mahrez would usually offer, and he was excellent. He starts the move for his goal, great movement, and he's got a fantastic left foot, driving it past Ruddy. Norwich made a great fist of the comeback, but it wasn't to be for them today.'

Jamie's performance was all the more impressive given that he was playing with two broken bones in his wrist. He refused to let the injury affect his game and was his usual livewire, fox-in-the-box pest as well as running at Norwich with pace and purpose on to balls delivered just outside the box. He was a menace throughout and almost impossible to defend against. The boy was rapidly becoming a striker worthy of the phrase 'top-class' and it was encouraging for Leicester and England that he was still developing and, just as importantly, still willing to learn and progress.

The *Daily Mirror* also paid tribute to Vardy for playing as if his broken wrist was an irrelevance to him, saying, 'Playing with a broken wrist really isn't bothering the Leicester striker. He dispatched the penalty with utter belief to make it six goals in five club matches, and the first time he has scored in five games in a row in league football. Eyebrows continue to be raised at his inclusion in the England squad just three years after he was playing league football, but Three Lions fans can do a lot worse than a hard-working, tireless runner with an eye for goal and total confidence from the penalty spot.'

Winger Schlupp, who was also on the scoresheet, stressed

the importance of Jamie to the team and how much of a nightmare he was to play against for opposing defenders. He said, 'Everyone has seen that we don't lack the fight and team spirit. We can dig deep when we need to. We can adapt to any situation. Jamie Vardy up front terrorises the defenders. He is a pest and is always in the defenders' faces.'

The fans were also delighted with the way Vardy continued to terrorise defences – and how far he had come since his non-league days. One fan, George, said, 'What strikes me as significant about Vardy is that he was playing non-league only a few years ago. I wonder how many more diamonds are there waiting a chance that will rarely if ever come while the clubs import poor or mediocre players from abroad. Really pleased for him, and I hope it continues. He's fresh, vibrant, energetic and persistent.'

Ranieri also had a wry smile when it was pointed out to him that Leicester remained in the top four – and the Champions League places – after the win. He said it meant they were still on target to achieve their season's aim of reaching forty points – which would mean safety from relegation! The boss told the BBC, 'We responded very well after our defeat against Arsenal. We showed good character and it was a good performance. We have fifteen points, twenty-five less than we need to. After we get that, we will see what happens.'

I was told that Vardy and his teammates loved the Italian and his sense of humour. They also loved the way he kept the spotlight and stress off them as they chased an unlikely Champions League spot with his talk of the forty-point target.

If Vardy had been the playing surprise of the 2015–16 season with his goals run, Ranieri had been his counterpart in management. The way he cajoled and looked after his players, and refused to revert to his 'Tinkerman' label, had been vital in the Foxes' amazing spurt to the top four. He deserved total respect for that and I was told he certainly had that in buckets off Jamie and his teammates. They had loved working with his predecessor Nigel Pearson but they adored this man just as much, if not more. Ranieri, Vardy and Leicester were a perfect fit and it showed in Jamie's outstanding performances and the team's outstanding results.

He had scored five on the trot but still there was little talk of his chasing Van Nistelrooy's record – although *The Mail on Sunday* pointed out that he was on the trail of one set at Leicester itself, adding, 'The probability is that Jamie Vardy does not indulge in much history reading. It is likely the name of Arthur Rowley, one of Leicester's goalscoring greats, has not registered on the new hero's radar. That is until now. Yesterday's goal – Vardy's sixth in five Premier League games – means he will be hearing quite a bit about Rowley, a man to score 251 in 303 league games and holder of a 58-year record the new England international is now breathing heavily down. Vardy will not have been notified [of] Rowley's blistering seven-game streak in the 1956–57 season; you can bet he'll be made aware of it after this.'

Jamie was in hot form and confident he could continue his goalscoring run. He never allowed it to become an obsession; indeed he would always maintain it was a bonus rather than the main aim. The team had to come first. In between his Premier League exploits he now picked up two caps for England in the Euro 2016 qualifiers against Estonia and Lithuania. After the international break – during which he drew a blank in front of goal – it was back down to the bread-and-butter business of the Premier League and a trip to the St Mary's stadium in Southampton. The Saints, under Dutch boss Ronald Koeman, had become the surprise package of the previous season – much like Leicester in the present campaign – and they would be a difficult challenge on their home turf.

And so it proved. The Foxes came away with a 2–2 draw after once again going two goals down away from home. If the defensive frailties were a long-term worry for Ranieri, at least he knew that his attack would always come up with the goods when called upon. Jamie was on target twice to earn a spoil of the points and to continue his run towards the record.

This was the sixth game in succession that he had netted for the club. His opener came in the sixty-fifth minute as he directed a Nathan Dyer cross into the bottom of the net, beyond the reach of Saints keeper Kelvin Davis. In injury time he claimed his second, rifling the ball home after a through ball from Mahrez. Afterwards, Ranieri was once again generous in his praise of his star man, telling reporters, 'We have fantastic spirit. We believe everything could be possible. We created a lot of chances. It is important to have good players on the bench and I have very good players who can change the match. Jamie Vardy is very important for us. If I was a player, I would be thinking, "Jamie can score, Jamie can score." I believe in this team. When we are desperate we make more, more and more.'

The two goals took Vardy's tally for the season to nine and meant he was the Premier League's top scorer. My friends at *The Sunday Times* summed up the impact Vardy was having on the top flight and how even rival boss Koeman had been impressed by his work rate and efforts, saying, 'Vardy epitomises City's blue-collar virtues, a striker who has graduated from non-league to international status in a matter of a few seasons, whose aggression and work ethic lifts spirits and terrifies opponents. His eighth and ninth goals of the season kept him as the league's leading scorer, but he has now scored in his last six league games. "He's strong, he's aggressive, he has great fighting spirit, I like him," said the manager. Nothing strange about that, except that the manager was Southampton's Ronald Koeman.'

Vardy made it a magnificent seven on the trot in the next game, the home fixture against Crystal Palace. His goal on the hour was enough to secure the points for City and keep him on track for the record. He pounced in the box after another assist from Mahrez; the deadly duo were tearing up defences throughout the Premier League and making a real name for themselves. At last, Jamie was getting most of the plaudits as he stole the headlines with his goals run, but Riyad was also proving a reliable scorer and a wizard on the wing. Some pundits were even comparing him to the legend that is Ryan Giggs – and some were suggesting the United manager-in-waiting would love to have him at Old Trafford to work with. Not that Leicester fans were at all enamoured by that scenario.

The goal meant that Jamie was now on a par with seven other players, four of them Englishmen who had scored seven in a row: Alan Shearer, Ian Wright, Mark Stein and Daniel Sturridge. The goal had been Vardy's only clear-cut chance of the game and he took it with aplomb. Ranieri once again applauded him, saying, 'He is in great form, he believes. He believes that every ball can be a good ball. It's a big achievement for him. It's a big achievement for us and also for our fans. It was a tough match, a battle for us. We battled well and deserved to win. We still take it step by step – it is important for us to reach forty points; that remains our first goal.'

Maybe so, but people were now talking openly about the Foxes as potential European candidates and Vardy as the season's potential top scorer in the top flight. He already had ten goals and was No. 1 in the chart. Talk of simply avoiding the drop into the Championship was cute by Ranieri, but it clearly wasn't going to happen. City were fifth in the table and, as one fan pointed out, Vardy had 'scored more goals in the past few weeks than Wayne Rooney had scored in the whole of 2015'.

Vardy himself told the press afterwards he had not realised he had added his name to the history books by scoring seven in seven, adding, 'I've not had many chances in the game so to get the goal that counts was important. I've just been told I've joined an elite group. Now it's on to the next one, on to the training ground, then the League Cup game against Hull in midweek, and then we prepare for next week's fixture. You saw how we defended at the end, great resilience. I still pinch myself every day. I've now managed to score ten goals in ten games so, hopefully, I can kick on again and we'll see where I end up.' He had also become the first Leicester player since the aforementioned Arthur Rowley in 1956–7 to strike in seven successive games.

And his efforts and those of his teammates meant Ranieri owed each of them a pizza, after promising he would 'get them in' if the team managed to keep a clean sheet against Palace. Jamie added, 'We've got a clean sheet so the gaffer can go and buy us pizzas. We'll definitely enjoy them. The gaffer's been saying he wants to buy them so I'll definitely make sure he does.' To which Ranieri replied, 'I will let Jamie have one-and-a-half pizzas! He is a player the fans love. He is in great form, believes in himself and it's important he stayed patient to get his goal.'

A week later Jamie was celebrating eight goals in eight games as his form of a lifetime continued. This time the victims were West Brom at the Hawthorns – always a tough place to go, in many ways like Stoke used to be under Tony Pulis. Now managed by Pulis, the Baggies had a similar do-or-die, dogs-of-war mentality. They would push you to the limit – and then beyond. Survivalists of the highest calibre, like all Pulis's teams down the ages, they never gave in, and never gave up. While Vardy took the headlines with his eighth in eight, it was Mahrez who was Albion's main undoing as he grabbed a brace and tormented them all afternoon with his mazy dribbles and inherent talent to find his teammates with pinpoint passes and crosses.

Vardy's goal was typical of his and Leicester's season, as he latched on to a through ball from a teammate and buried the ball in the bottom left-hand corner of the net with that lethal right foot. On this occasion, Danny Drinkwater was the provider as the duo raced through Albion's ranks. Speed and deadly finishing – the trademark of Vardy's season and his ever-increasing tally of goals.

After the game Ranieri once again praised his main man and, for the first time, now spoke publicly about the record Jamie was chasing. But he also told the assembled reporters that his team would not be treated to pizza again that night, as the defending had not been good enough. Claudio said, 'We fight to the end. We have a very strong character and play good football. I told my players they were playing very well at half-time, to be careful at set-plays, and it was important to move the ball quickly and put them under pressure. We did that well. It's important Jamie continues to work for the team. The record is good for everybody. Jamie is at the start of his career now and we have to wait. He's come from non-league. It's not too late to arrive at the highest level. I'm very happy with him, he's in great condition now. But if he scores goals, it's his job.

'I feel very good here at Leicester with the chairman, with the family of the chairman, with all my staff, with all our players, all our fans. It is fantastic, there is a good electricity. It's one of the best atmospheres I've had at any club. I am a very lucky man to be here.'

Ranieri smiled when asked if he would be treating Vardy to a pizza for his efforts. He shook his head and said, 'We conceded a goal today, so no pizza. Nothing.'

No pizza maybe, but it was one step closer to the dream for Vardy. What had started out as a goal glut that was helping Leicester maintain an unlikely push at the top of the Premier League was now turning into a one-man push for a place in the history books. Jamie said he still wasn't interested in talk of records, that the team still mattered most — and it was this attitude that was allowing him to pursue the dream. By distancing himself from talk of the record and refusing to engage in discussion of it, he was taking the pressure off himself that would have mounted if he was publicly going for it. I have no doubt that it did cross his mind now and again — he is human, after all, if superhuman in terms of goals — but he has an ability to compartmentalise issues. And the issue of the record was placed in a compartment firmly at the back of his mind.

Jamie simply focused on the team's effort once again when asked for his views after the win. He said, 'It was down to the character of the side. It's great to score goals but it's all about the team. We showed we had great character to come back after we were behind. We played well as a team.'

Even Tony Pulis was impressed after Jamie had destroyed his team at the Hawthorns. The West Brom boss told a press conference, 'Credit to Leicester. They played to their strengths, Jamie Vardy is a handful, he's on fire and he caused us problems. Vardy is an exceptional player. His pace frightened us all afternoon.'

Gary Lineker also commented on Vardy's exploits, tweeting, 'Vardy strikes for the 8th consecutive Premier League game. Game's gone mad!'

If Vardy himself was refusing to bow to the pressure linking him with Van Nistelrooy's record, the chatter in the background was becoming louder and louder as the Fleet Street sports desks started to build up their coverage of it. The *Daily Mail*, for instance, commented after the Albion match, 'He stayed long after the final whistle to milk the applause of the Leicester fans. Jamie Vardy scores when he wants, they sang, and on this form it's hard to disagree. The England striker's decisive effort in a five-goal thriller at the Hawthorns means he has scored in eight successive Premier League games, eclipsing the likes of Alan Shearer and Thierry Henry. Having equalled the achievements of Liverpool's Daniel Sturridge, Vardy is two behind record-holder Ruud van Nistelrooy for Manchester United.'

And my friends at *The Sun* also took note of the record – while at the same time arguing that Vardy now deserved much more credit as a striker of international class, saying, 'Let's end the talk now over whether Jamie Vardy is England class. It's time to start a whole new debate. Who would you rather have leading the line for your team? Robert Lewandowski, Thomas Muller, Sergio Aguero or . . . Jamie Vardy? The one-time Fleetwood forward scored what turned out to be Leicester's winner as he battered down the hallowed doors of the Premier League's goal-scoring Hall of Fame. Seldom has a player deserved it more than 28-year-old Vardy as he joined Liverpool's Daniel Sturridge to score in his eighth consecutive game just when it looked as if West Brom would frustrate him.'

The Sun pointed out that not only was Jamie on Van Nistelrooy's trail, he was more than likely to nab his record if he continued this brilliant run of form. The boy was a goal machine and no rivals had yet found the way to stop him in his tracks.

And even the more conservative *Daily Telegraph* was at pains to stress that Vardy was on the trail of Van Nistelrooy – and looking unstoppable as he aimed for the record. It reported that, 'Jamie Vardy cannot have envisaged matching a record set by Ruud Van Nistelrooy when he was playing on the gnarled battlefields of non-league. Yet the Leicester City forward is now inching closer to Van Nistelrooy's remarkable streak from 2003 after scoring for the eighth Premier League game in a row to settle an absorbing encounter at the Hawthorns. Van Nistelrooy, the former Manchester United striker, scored in ten successive league games 12 years ago and Vardy simply appears unstoppable on current form, with his 77th minute strike proving the crucial goal. Few would bet against him at least equalling that achievement, with games against Watford and Newcastle up next.'

The fans were also backing Jamie to take the record, and urging him to do so.

Lifelong Foxes fan Joe Ritchie said, 'It's brilliant what Jamie has achieved this season and I've no doubts at all that he can take the record. He's scoring for fun and he can't stop. With Mahrez helping him and also scoring I'm sure we can keep up this good run and that Jamie will do it. It's brilliant what's happened this season after the struggles of last season. Ranieri has been a revelation – and so has Vardy. When Pearson was sacked I was worried we'd be in another relegation battle but it's not been like that at all. It has been the absolute opposite, in fact, and you can't ask for much more than that. All power to Vardy and Ranieri!'

And England fan 'John' urged England boss Roy Hodgson to take note, too. He said, 'With Vardy in such brilliant form, how can Hodgson ignore him for the big games now? Take him to the Euros in summer, Roy, he might just save your job!'

He might do just that – assuming Hodgson has the nous to take him. The England manager is inherently conservative, so there were no guarantees as this book went to the printers in February 2016; we could but hope.

In the next chapter, we'll see how Vardy inched ever closer to the record, and take a look at how his route to the top ten compares with Van Nistelrooy's – and salute Jamie for surpassing the Dutch legend when he grabbed that almost unbelievable eleventh goal in eleven games.

Right: Vardy playing for Fleetwood Town in 2011, shortly after he was signed to the club. He scored 31 league goals during his first season here, and won the teams Player of the Year award as they won the division.

Left: Vardy celebrates scoring his side's first goal of the game with his team mates against Middlesbrough in 2012.

Above left: David Nugent celebrates with Jamie Vardy following their 4–1 win over Derby County during the Sky Bet Championship match at the King Power Stadium, cementing their lead at the top of the table.

Above right: Vardy's Premier League debut. Leicester played against Arsenal and finished with a 1–1 draw.

Below: On 21 September 2014, Vardy delivered a Man of the Match performance by scoring his first Premier League goal and setting up the other four as Leicester produced a 5–3 victory against Manchester United.

Above: Jamie celebrates with his team mates after scoring Leicester's first goal of the 2015-2016 season in a match against Sunderland. They went on to win the match 4–2.

Below: Jamie Vardy (front left) in his second appearance in the England team. He played against San Marino in the UEFA Euro 2016 Qualifiers.

Above: The Leicester City team celebrate Vardy scoring in 11 consecutive games, setting a new Premier League record.

Below: Vardy scores both goals in a 2–0 win against Liverpool, the first being a long-distance volley described as 'world-class' by Liverpool manager Jürgen Klopp.

CHAPTER TEN

ON CLOUD NINE

Jamie had made it eight in eight games with his goal at the Hawthorns at the end of October 2015. The pundits, fans and players were all starting to really sit up and take note of his exploits and the talk in the pubs and on the terraces was whether he could keep his cool and match, or even surpass, Ruud's record – or whether he would crack under the pressure. As we have already seen, it was unlikely he would crack under the stress of it all – as he simply refused to accept there was any pressure. As far as Vardy was concerned, the only people getting hot under the collar were those outside Leicester City FC. Certainly he was not putting himself under any, as he continued to maintain that the main thing was how the team played and how the team fared. Any personal glory was purely incidental: he would always maintain he was a team player first.

But there was little doubt that the headlines regarding the record were growing every day and when he scored a week later, for the ninth time in a row in the Premier League, they reached saturation point. It became more than *a* talking point: it became *the* talking point across the country. That No. 9 goal came in the game at the King Power Stadium against a team many had considered would be a fellow relegation battler with the Foxes. But, like City, Watford had proved people wrong. And, like City, they had done so by playing entertaining, attacking football rather than 'parking the bus', as many pundits had predicted. The Hornets were a credit to the game and another surprise package in this season of surprises in the English top flight.

Not that it should have perhaps been such a surprise given the positive nature of their manager. Quique Sanchez Flores was a former Atlético Madrid coach and led them to the Europa League title in 2010. As a player, he starred at Real Madrid and took charge of their youth team in 2001. His godfather was Real legend Alfredo Di Stefano, so it was hardly a shock that he liked his teams to perform with verve and ambition. It meant the match with Leicester, which many fans would have considered a turn-off a couple of seasons earlier, was now anticipated with a certain relish. Given the form of the teams, their managers and the attacking football both encouraged, it had the makings of a fine afternoon's football.

Before kick-off Vardy revealed how modern technology was helping him become the league's top scorer. He admitted that his iPad had played a key role, telling reporters, 'We get given all the videos on an iPad to watch, to see what the opposition defence is like. You watch videos, then take that out onto the training pitch and try to put it into practice. I'm not really looking at the record. There's still a way to go. I'll get back on the training field and look at how I can break Watford's defence and hopefully get another goal – or maybe two. Then I'll look at the next game after that.'

He was working hard on his game and felt it was paying off. He had the feeling he could score any time, anyplace, anywhere – a feeling that had led to some players labelling him 'the Martini man'. This was a reference to the old Martini slogan, famous in the 1980s as the advertising men tried to sell the alcoholic tipple to a British audience on TV. 'My confidence couldn't be higher,' he said. 'Now I'm going into games thinking, "I *will* score today." That's how every striker should feel, otherwise there's no point in being a striker. It's as simple as that. That's what I get paid for – putting the ball in the back of the net. There's no feeling like it at the moment. Everything I touch seems to be going in. Long may that continue.'

And he maintained the record was still not dominating his thoughts, adding, 'All that's at the back of my mind is getting a goal and three points. I remember Van Nistelrooy scoring loads of goals for Manchester United, but you don't really remember seeing them coming in consecutive games. With the amount of goals he scored, you'd probably think he'd scored in more successive games. But I've not really looked at stats like that. All I've thought about is getting as many goals as I can for Leicester.'

His boss Ranieri had become a little concerned that England head coach Roy Hodgson had spoken publicly about Jamie, saying the boy 'should not expect to play down the middle'. Hodgson told a press conference, 'An England shirt is a very valuable commodity. When you've only played two games you are in no position to go to the coach and say, "I will play for England but only in this position." At this early stage in his international career he should be happy to be in the squad, even happier if he's playing. He should be trying to convince us he has the ability to play as a forward in the England team. He mustn't get too hung up that he will only be good if he plays "here".

'The player everyone is interested in can be fleeting. When I pick a squad, I don't pick them on what the mass media or social media say. I pick them on their abilities and what they can do for England. We believe in Jamie Vardy,' said Hodgson. 'When we selected him, I don't think there were a lot of people saying, "Fantastic, that's a great idea, Jamie Vardy is the obvious man." Now there are. He's the top goalscorer and has a record at his fingertips. We think he's a very good player and hope he continues. But Jamie has only played a couple of games from the start.'

Hodgson's comments were all very well and good if Vardy had publicly complained about his role for the national team – but he hadn't. If I hadn't been aware of that, the comments would have suggested to me that Jamie was getting above himself, and playing the big shot. But he would be the last person to go around shouting the odds. This was, let's remember, the boy from nowhere, who had made it in the Premier League from non-league, and now to England. He was simply grateful – and honoured – to have even been in a position to represent his country.

That he was in such a position was nothing short of a miracle, yes, a story Hollywood would be proud of, but one you wouldn't really imagine could be true in the modern era of the game, with its billions of pounds at stake and its domination by players who cost the earth to buy, and just as much to pay.

The fans were just as puzzled as to why Hodgson was making a problem where there wasn't one. One England fan said, 'I'm totally confused, I'd like to know when Vardy made those statements. In what other country does a manager not play the players who are in form? Then people wonder why England is the laughing stock of the football world.'

Another said, 'Just get him onto the team, Roy. Vardy has more pace and could strike! He puts dedication [*sic*] than Rooney, sorry but it's true.'

While a third fan, quite rightly in my opinion, questioned why Vardy was not considered for a central role, when a misfiring Rooney was a shoo-in, saying, 'Why is Rooney in the England line-up? Vardy's on his way to breaking records.'

Vardy's club boss Ranieri waded into the row when he said he believed he should play down the middle for England, Ranieri said, 'It's difficult because I am not Roy. Roy knows his team very well and tries to put in his squad the best players. For me it is the same at Leicester. I have some players and I want to put them in the best position for them, the team and everybody. I think Jamie has to be free in my opinion. When he is free he is amazing but we play with two strikers, not with one, and I am not Roy. I respect him and his shape, but in my team Jamie plays as a free forward. Jamie is an intelligent player and whatever Roy Hodgson asks him to do for the team, he will try to do. He is not selfish.'

I agree with Claudio and I have to say it wasn't the first time Hodgson had erred by publicly castigating his England players when there was no need. I remember early in Ross Barkley's national team career that he was publicly taken to task for needlessly losing the ball in central midfield. Of course, no one is saying that Hodgson shouldn't pull up his men for slack play, but a public dressing down? Surely, it would have been better left said in the dressing room, a quiet word in the player's ear. Similarly, I don't see how Vardy being told publicly that he was out of order thinking he was an automatic choice down the middle for England helped the player. Especially as I still cannot find any trace of Jamie making such a demand in the public arena.

Despite the furore around his embryonic England career, Jamie was his usual cool, calm self as he arrived at the King Power Stadium for the clash with Watford that could take him a goal closer to the Van Nistelrooy record. Yet it would prove to be something of a comedy of errors rather than the attacking feast we had anticipated. Watford keeper Heurelho Gomes proved to be the joker-in-chief, which was fortunate for Leicester and Vardy. In the first instance, he gifted City their opener when he messed up a weak effort by N'Golo Kanté, fumbling the ball into the net, and then he brought down Vardy in the box for a penalty, the man on a goals mission making no mistake from the spot. He claimed his ninth in nine gratefully and saluted the City fans, who in turn began their now familiar refrain, 'Jamie Vardy's having a party!'

Leicester themselves entered the errors register when Kanté brought down Juan Carlos Paredes in the box, and Troy Deeney stepped up to convert his spot-kick. It all made for a tense finish but it was one Ranieri could have done without. City held on and notched their seventh win of the season and the victory put them joint top of the Premier League table with Arsenal and Manchester City.

Plus, of course, Jamie was now just one goal from matching Van Nistelrooy's twelve-year record haul. And let's not forget that Vardy had actually already made the record books, as his nine goals had all come in the same season – whereas Ruud's had been split across the end of one season and the start of another in 2003.

It was rival boss Flores who led the praise, saying Vardy was 'the best striker we have faced so far'. That was praise indeed from the Watford chief, since his team had already come up against Kun Agüero and Alexis Sánchez. Vardy had been called up by Roy Hodgson for England's forthcoming friendlies against Spain and France and many pundits and players believed he was ready to start for his country.

His teammate Danny Drinkwater was convinced that Jamie was now international class and fully deserved his call-up, saying, 'Scoring nine games in a row is world-class-striker stuff and he deserves to be part of the international scene. His biggest threat is when he plays down the middle.'

BBC Sport's John Hartson, the former West Ham and Celtic striker, agreed, saying, 'Vardy's form is incredible. If he's fit and raring to go, he should start for England.'

Ranieri was also of the same opinion, while still attempting to cool talk of City remaining as top four contenders. He said, 'We could not have imagined this, but it is only November. It's not May. We still have to achieve forty points first. Jamie is fantastic. He'll be fit for England. After the goal he continued to run and fight – he's okay. What more can I say about Jamie? I want to talk about the great moment when Riyad gave Jamie the ball for the penalty. To see Riyad do that says everything about the spirit of this team. It is important to continue the momentum. It's not easy for us, but we are very ambitious.'

To use a footballing cliché, the fans were also 'over the moon' at the way the season was panning out. Their team were pushing for a Champions League spot and their No. 9 was pushing to claim an all-time consecutive goals record. As one City fan said, 'This is wonderful, amazing and awesome for the City to be third in the top league in English football after twelve matches. For Vardy, a Leicester City player to be on the verge of becoming a Premier League legend is priceless. I have to keep pinching myself to make sure I'm awake and not dreaming. A question. Has Leicester City *ever* been in a similar position? In the meantime, *live the dream!*'

Another said, 'Every week is becoming a new dream. [I] keep asking my missus to look up the scores in case I can't read and I'm smiling for nothing. This is just magic. Can't wait for the next chapter!'

One fan was already looking ahead to Vardy equalling and claiming the record, saying, 'Watching Newcastle last night on MOTD. Vardy's gonna get a hat-trick up there – which means beating the record against the team [Man United] who set it is even more special than any of us could of imagined.'

And another agreed entirely with those sentiments, and was excited by the prospect of the big games looming. 'What a time to be a City fan,' he enthused. 'Joint top of the league and now only five wins needed to be sure of Prem football next year, with all the money that brings. Delightful attacking football and, despite coaches telling the opposition how to stop us, they still haven't found a way. Cannot wait for the Man Utd and Chelski games – *no fear*!'

It was certainly heady stuff and who could begrudge the loyal City fans for enjoying the high life after the previous season's troubles and toil?

The players themselves were relishing every minute of the campaign as they continued to prove wrong the pundits who said they would be 'down with the Christmas decorations' come the New Year. There had been no sign yet of a downturn; this run by Vardy and the team was proving to be much more than a flash in the pan.

More vindication of their form came soon after the win over Watford, when Vardy was named Barclays Premier League Player of the Month. He collected the award on 10 November, although it was for his exploits in October. He hit five goals in four Premier League matches for Leicester that month and it was the first time Jamie had won the trophy. He had to see off the challenge of some top contenders to seal the win – Arsenal midfielder Mesut Özil and striker Olivier Giroud, Manchester City midfielder Kevin De Bruyne, Watford striker Odion Ighalo and Stoke City's brilliant young goalkeeper Jack Butland.

Leicester fans had been hoping boss Ranieri would join him as a winner, but he lost out for the Manager of the Month award to Arsenal's Arsène Wenger. City had won three games and drawn one that month while the Gunners had won all four of theirs, so Wenger had just edged it.

A month later Ranieri would get his reward as he was named Manager of the Month for November – with Jamie retaining his award as Player of the Month. The Barclays Premier League issued a statement congratulating both of them, saying, 'Vardy became the fourth man to win successive Barclays Player of the Month awards, following Dennis Bergkamp (August and September 1997), Cristiano Ronaldo (November and December 2006) and Harry Kane (January and February 2015). Ranieri picked up the manager's accolade for the third time, having won it with Chelsea in September 2003 and March 2004.

'This is the second time a Leicester player and manager have won the monthly awards "double", after Peter Taylor and Tim Flowers did so in September 2000.

'In November, the Foxes beat Watford 2–1 and Newcastle United 3–0 before earning a 1–1 draw with Manchester United that put them level on points with Manchester City at the top of the Barclays Premier League, and they have continued their remarkable start to the campaign by going two points clear at the summit ahead of this weekend's matches. Vardy scored once in each of those three matches, and his strike against Man Utd at the King Power Stadium made him the first man to score in 11 consecutive BPL fixtures. The Leicester forward is leading the race for the 2015/16 Barclays Golden Boot with 14 top-flight goals, three clear of nearest challenger Romelu Lukaku.'

Indeed he was. That goal against Watford had put him on the brink of Van Nistelrooy's record and, as the Premier League's press statement for his and Ranieri's double award outlined, he had finally surpassed Ruud's record against Man United at the King Power in November. We have already looked at how he did just that in the previous chapter – while outlining how he snapped up the initial nine in this one. Before moving on to the subject of his England breakthrough, let's take a swift look at how Van Nistelrooy himself set the record, with a few comparisons to Jamie's achievement.

Overall, you would have to say that Jamie's was the finer achievement in that he obviously eventually surpassed Ruud's ten in ten with his eleven in eleven, but also because the Dutchman was playing in a far superior team. That is no slight on Leicester or their players in the 2015–16 campaign. It is just that Van Nistelrooy was surrounded by world-class stars, as we have touched upon before, such as Beckham and Giggs, who made it easier for him to snap up his goals. I would contend that Vardy would have scored many more goals in a team containing such renowned players. Of course, in the likes of Mahrez he did have one teammate who could be called a potentially world-class star. But he certainly wasn't surrounded by them as Ruud was.

Even Roy Keane, one of football's toughest men to impress, admitted that he was spellbound by Van Nistelrooy's goal-scoring ability and run. The Irishman said that he was one of the greatest goalscorers of all time. In his second autobiography, Keane wrote, 'When Ruud was going through one on one, I never doubted him. Some players would be going, "Fucking hell, hard and low? Or dink it over?" But when Ruud was through there might as well have been no goalkeeper.'

Ruud and Jamie share that simplicity of scoring – both poachers, both men who liked to speed away from opponents and both deadly in the box. Ruud's ten-goal run came against Fulham, Liverpool, Newcastle in two separate games, Arsenal, Blackburn Rovers, Tottenham, Charlton, Everton and Bolton. It is a telling fact that all ten goals by Ruud were delivered within the box. Ruud began his run with a hat-trick in the 3–0 home win over Fulham on 22 March 2003. The first goal – the one that started the goals glut – was a penalty. On 5 April, he followed up with a brace in the 4–0 home win over Liverpool, again the first of which was a penalty. A week later Ruud was on target for the third successive match as United won 6–2 at Newcastle. And for the third successive game he scored from a penalty.

On 16 April, he grabbed his fourth in four with a fine finish in the 2–2 draw at Arsenal. Three days later Ruud made it a famous five with a headed goal as United overwhelmed Blackburn 3–1 at Old Trafford.

It was the end of April 2003, and Ruud scored his sixth in six with a well-placed right-foot shot in the 2–0 win at Tottenham.

At the start of May he notched his second hat-trick in his brilliant run into the record books, the first goal coming as he left the hapless Charlton backline for dead before prodding the ball home in front of the adoring faithful at Old Trafford.

Ruud's eighth in eight came in the last game of the 2002–3 season, with a fourth penalty on his run, this time as Everton were put to the sword as United triumphed 2–1 at Goodison Park to complete a superb season's work that had seen them win their fifteenth Premier League crown under a delighted Alex Ferguson. United won the title by five points and it was Van Nistelrooy who had led the charge with his goals.

Yet, in a less talented team, Vardy had pushed Leicester into the top four of the Premier League on his goals run. I still maintain that his was the greater achievement – especially as the goals all came in one season, and in the first part of one of the most competitive seasons in memory at that. A season when the likes of Chelsea found themselves in a relegation struggle at times and one in which the likes of Leicester, West Ham and Stoke prospered. All three of those unlikely teams had their own key men, who propelled them to an even more unlikely push for glory: the Hammers had Dimitri Payet while Stoke had Xherdan Shaqiri – and the Foxes, of course, had Vardy and Mahrez.

Van Nistelrooy, meanwhile, would get the two remaining goals he needed to set that ten-successive-goals record at the start of the following campaign, the 2003–4 season. The ninth goal came in United's 4–0 rout of Bolton on 16 August 2003, the first day of the new season, another shot hammered home, and the tenth arrived as the Red Devils won 2–1 at Newcastle a week later. It came from another right-footed shot – as all the others on the run did apart from his headed goal against Blackburn. Like Vardy, Ruud was right-footed and, like Vardy, he used his foot brilliantly – it was a goal-scoring weapon.

Louis van Gaal, United manager when Vardy completed his record, said he believed both men deserved equal credit for their achievements and noted that they had comparable assets in that both regularly were 'running in behind the defence and you can compare them'. Before the match in which Vardy would break Ruud's record, Van Gaal added that he saw Jamie as a 'nasty' threat to his team, telling reporters, 'He was last season a very nasty player for us. He scored, won a penalty, and now he is scoring ten games in a row, then you are a great player. I only know Dennis Bergkamp as a player who did the same with Ajax. It's not so easy to do that. Vardy is a player who is difficult to defend. It shall be difficult, I think, but we can do that because we have a lot of clean sheets already.'

Of course, he was proved wrong on that last point – as Jamie hit the record-claiming goal against United! And the debate over whether Vardy or Ruud most deserves credit for their record goals runs will be one that lasts for years. Footie fans across the country, and abroad, weighed in with contributions with most, I have to say, siding with my view that Jamie deserved more credit, given the circumstances in which he set the new record.

One fan said, 'The team Vardy is playing in and the fact he is nowhere near the calibre of Van Nistelrooy makes me go for him. I was a big fan of Van Nistelrooy and remember that streak – he was terrific. I knew at some point though it would be broken because ten games while amazing is more achievable than say Messi's record of twenty-one, which might never be outdone. I'd like to see Vardy break it because for someone who has come from non-league, to do what he has is sensational.'

Even a United fan backed Vardy with Reds supporter Ammar maintaining, 'Even as a United fan, I'd have to say Vardy because of the teams the two competitors played in.'

While 'Bill' agreed with my view that Vardy's achievement was more commendable, as he did not have a whole team of world-class players backing up his attempt on the record, he added, 'What Vardy has done is absolutely brilliant. He is not playing for a big team but he still manages to do that. He is not at Ruud's level and he is not playing for a team who, at that time in 2003, were one of the best in the world. So Vardy's achievement is better.'

And there you have it. The story of how a non-league player made it into the big league and matched and then surpassed the goal-scoring record of one of the most prolific strikers in Premier League history. How the boy from nowhere got one over on Ruud van Nistelrooy, one of Manchester United and Holland's greatest centre-forwards ever. It is some story – and some achievement. Little wonder that after Jamie had secured the record, renowned screenwriter Adrian Butchart said he would love to make a biopic about Jamie's remarkable life story – about his meteoric rise from footballing obscurity to record-breaker and icon.

Butchart, part of the team behind the *Goal!* movies, even suggested likely Hollywood stars to play Vardy. I was told by a reliable source that Jamie was 'well chuffed' that the likes of Robert Pattinson, Zac Efron and Andrew Garfield had been suggested for the starring role! Butchart told my friends at *The Sun*, 'It's the kind of story that, if we made it up, people wouldn't believe it. His achievements are incredible and to break the Premier League record with such a sublime goal against the biggest club in football pushed him to the top of our agenda.

'It's amazing to think he was playing non-league football and making medical splints for a living until so recently before breaking the record. It is the kind of role actors dream of.'

And that is without taking into account Vardy's increasing involvement in the England squad – another unbelievable breakthrough which we will detail in the next chapter.

CHAPTER ELEVEN

ENGLAND EXPECTS

The icing on the cake for Jamie came when he was called up for the England squad for the first time in 2015. It crowned his achievement of emerging from nowhere – non-league obscurity – to global fame within the shortest of timeframes. It was another chapter in a story that, as we keep saying, you would not believe if someone told you it was a film script. From Fleetwood to playing alongside Wayne Rooney in an England shirt? No way! Tell us another one. But this was very real and Jamie was 'delighted, proud and honoured' to have made it to the very top of the tree.

He looked smart and distinctive in his England blazer as he joined up with the squad, the cream of the crop, for the first time and fitted in nicely with his teammates. Welcomed to the fold by the captain, Rooney, Jamie was soon laughing and joking with other squad members. He did not look at all out of place and impressed in training with his speed, shooting skills and obvious ability to pick up what the coaches expected of him.

Vardy had one great advantage over other stars in the squad in that he had no big ego. He was Jamie Vardy from Sheffield, who had made it against the odds and he was determined to enjoy and savour his time with England. Vardy had always maintained he was a team player first and foremost and now he would show it by fitting in where boss Roy Hodgson asked him to go and working hard for a starring role. He would never complain about where he was played – despite what Hodgson had seemed to imply in one press conference. Indeed, he just felt lucky and privileged to be part of the setup, full stop.

It was a dream come true: every footballer of English blood dreamed of playing one day for his country. Now Vardy was on the very verge of that; it was something he had dreamt of but it had been a pipe dream when he had been turning out in non-league on muddy, waterlogged pitches in the freezing cold, with just a cup of tea and a biscuit as a half-time treat and a wait for his turn in the showers at full-time. Now everything was top-class – from the remarkable facilities at St George's Park, where the team trained and stayed in absolute luxury, to those at arguably the best stadium in world football today, yes, the new Wembley. This was the world of the privileged and the pampered and Jamie Vardy sometimes had to pinch himself to believe this was happening to him. A confident character? Of course. But a fantasist? Never, always the realist – but this was pure fantasy. Beyond his wildest dreams – and then some, too.

He was training with the elite and staying in the best hotels with everything you could need available night and day. It didn't get much better than this and Jamie was absolutely determined that he would not only take his chance, but that he would make it impossible for Hodgson to drop him from the squad. His new dream was to make the squad for the Euro 2016 championships to be held in France the following summer. Even that would take some doing – but then he had overcome every previous obstacle on his way to the top, so why should he not do so now? It was likely that Hodgson would choose four strikers as part of his twenty-three-man squad for the finals and some were guaranteed places, if they were sufficiently fit. There would be Rooney, Harry Kane and Daniel Sturridge, assuming the last of these could end his ongoing injury nightmare. That would leave just one place available on the plane – and it would most likely be between him, Danny Welbeck and Andy Carroll to claim it. Welbeck was a favourite of Hodgson and Carroll could stake a claim as the 'alternative candidate'. Carroll was the battering-ram option who could be brought on late in a game to bully the opposition and unsettle them. He would be useful if England were chasing the game and, given all that, was a genuine candidate for that fourth striker's spot on the plane. So it would be a battle to dislodge one of these men if Jamie was to make it to France.

Six candidates for four slots. Of course, there was always the possibility that Carroll and Sturridge would drop out through injury – or that Hodgson would consider taking them to be a gamble because they *might* fall foul of injury. That would open the door to Vardy and Welbeck joining Rooney and Kane in the final reckoning. But nothing was certain and, as Jamie Vardy saw it, the best approach would be to assume that all of them would be fit and so he would have to battle for a spot on merit alone.

It wouldn't be easy but he had come this far under his own steam and he was committed to giving everything so he would be part of Hodgson's plans for France. He had one foot in the door already, in that one of his biggest admirers was Hodgson's assistant head coach, Gary Neville. The former Man United full-back and skipper had become manager of Spanish La Liga side Valencia in 2015 and, according to the *Daily Star*, was urging his bosses at the club to snap up Vardy. The *Daily Star* claimed in December, 2015, that, 'Part of his [Neville's] role will be to advise Valencia owner and business associate Peter Lim on potential transfer targets in England. And top of Nev's shopping list will be Foxes sensation Vardy, who last weekend became the first Premier League striker to score in 11 consecutive games – beating Ruud van Nistelrooy's record of ten. But come the summer the situation may change with Foxes boss Claudio Ranieri unlikely to block a dream move to one of Europe's top outfits. That is when Valencia will enter the race – whether Neville is still at the helm or not. Having been integral in Vardy's England selection, Neville is in prime position to persuade the player to try his luck in Spain.'

A month earlier, before taking the Valencia job, Neville – in his role as a Sky Sports presenter – had outlined why he liked Vardy and how he had watched him change from a hopeful into a star striker. Gary said, 'Any player who plays up front in a Premier League team needs to catch the eye of the England coaching team and the reports that were coming through twelve months ago were that he was raw, a little bit erratic in front of goal, but he was lightning quick and a bit of a handful. His England call-up probably gave him a lot more confidence. He's come into this season and he's a completely different player in terms of that little bit of rawness. He was unpolished last season, you look at him now and he's a fantastic finisher.'

Given his rise through the ranks from non-league, Vardy had no stepped introduction to the England first-team squad. He had not represented his country at Under-17, Under-19 or Under-21 level – the traditional route for the traditional elite footballer of the modern era. And he also missed out on playing for any England B teams or even the Great Britain Olympics team – again, he was an outsider looking in until he finally made the Premier League with Leicester. There would be no gentle introduction for Jamie – his arrival on the England scene would be late in the day. He was twenty-eight and straight into the squad in May 2015 as Hodgson prepared for two matches – a friendly in Dublin against the Republic of Ireland and a Euro 2016 qualifier away in Slovenia. Both were important games, the former a much-needed warm-up for the latter and a chance for the squad to gel after months apart. The latter was a key match in what was proving a successful qualifying campaign for Hodgson and his staff.

The FA announced Vardy's arrival along with two other newcomers in a press statement on 21 May 2015, which ran:

'Charlie Austin, Jamie Vardy and Tom Heaton are the three new names in Roy Hodgson's latest England squad. The Three Lions boss has selected a 24-man squad for two games next month – a friendly against Republic of Ireland in Dublin on 7 June and a Euro 2016 Qualifier against Slovenia in Ljubljana on 14 June. Burnley stopper Heaton, and strikers Austin from Queens Park Rangers and Leicester City's Vardy earn their first call-ups at senior level. Heaton, 29, has previous international experience for England having featured throughout the youth ranks from Under-16s to Under-21s. Former Burnley and Swindon hitman Austin, 25, has been called up after scoring 17 goals for the Hoops this season, as will 28-year-old Vardy, who helped the Foxes escape relegation this season. The trio come into a squad that has won seven and drawn one of their eight internationals this season.'

One interesting fact from that statement came with the ages of the three newcomers – Vardy, as we know, twenty-eight, Heaton, twenty-nine, and Austin, twenty-five. None were spring chickens, all had arrived on the international stage later than would normally be expected in their careers. It proved that, as the game progressed and players stayed fitter and more conditioned well into their twenties and beyond, age was becoming less of a barrier to elite selection. Ryan Giggs, another example, had played for Man United until he was forty, after looking after himself well with diet and regular yoga workouts, as well as performing his normal fitness routines.

So there was hope for footballers like Vardy that they could play for England for a good while if they maintained their fitness and talent – even if they had arrived late in the day. It was a breakthrough that meant others, maybe even in non-league like Vardy, could have a dream of one day playing for their country. Vardy's smashing down of the barriers had given hope to numerous others as they struggled to make the ranks of the elite pros. Age was now no limiter and neither was where you started or where you happened to be. You can dream and dream big. That was Vardy's magnificent legacy as he made the England squad that May. The boy from nowhere had truly arrived now.

A day after his squad selection Hodgson outlined his thinking to the press about his new boys, including Vardy, and how circumstances, particularly injuries, had allowed him to take a look at them. Roy told reporters, 'When you look at this squad, Daniel Sturridge is out, of course, who would normally be there. Danny Welbeck, we have fears about. We hope he's going to recover and that he will be available for Arsenal, certainly for the Cup Final. But we can't be certain of that because he hasn't played for a while and hasn't recovered from his knee injury yet. On top of that, there's Harry Kane and Saido Berahino, who have been with us, and Danny Ings, who probably would have been with us at least on a couple of occasions had it not been for Under-21 commitments.

'If we can confirm what we have seen with Charlie and Jamie, and they show they are capable of being international players too, then our talent pool up front will be surprisingly big, certainly if you compare with what was available three years ago.'

Hodgson then revealed that, rather surprisingly and touchingly, he had admired Vardy from afar for a few years, always hoping he would progress to such a high level. Roy had watched him play when he was boss at West Bromwich Albion. On a free day, he had travelled to Kidderminster to see Jamie play for Fleetwood in a non-league clash. As Roy explained, it was during his season at Fleetwood Town in the Conference Premier in 2011 that he first spotted Vardy, shortly before his switch to Leicester. He said, 'I was at West Brom and he was playing at Kidderminster, which wasn't so far from us. He was getting a lot of good reviews and it was an ideal opportunity to watch him play. It was a cold night, a difficult surface, and to be honest he didn't get a lot of chances to show what he could do – neither did anyone else for that matter. It was a very competitive Conference match but you could see then he had some ability. That was the first time I saw him but at the time we were monitoring players but not with a view specifically to sign him. Next thing I knew, he'd moved on and gone to Leicester and we have obviously followed him there. We think he has some interesting qualities and that this will be a chance to see them at close hand.'

It was soon time for the first training session and Vardy made the short journey from Leicester to St George's Park in Burton-on-Trent on Wednesday, 3 June. He was excited and ready to show what he could do. Nerves? He rarely suffered from them; he was a confident, assured individual and nothing fazed him. But even Jamie felt a few butterflies in his tummy as he arrived at England's training HQ. Not for long, though. After introductions and a few jokes from the regulars, he settled in and settled down for business. This was what he had worked so hard for; all those cold, character-making days in non-league, all the effort and sacrifices – no way was he going to blow it now.

Jamie told pals that the first two days of training went well and that he enjoyed the workouts and circuits and mixing with top players in the England setup. He liked working with fellow newcomer Charlie Austin, who had also had to fight like him to make it to the top. Charlie paid tribute to Jamie when speaking to the press about his own take on the opening sessions at St George's Park, saying, 'People from the lower leagues are still dreaming they can make the step up to play professionally and then play for the national team. I believe that people below us are looking at me and Jamie and see that it can be done. We bounce off each other and speak. I don't know the full story from Jamie's background. I know we both came from non-league, I played in the South and Jamie played in the North. Me and Jamie coming here gives people the opportunity if they work as hard as they can and achieve their dreams.'

That was an excellent insight – indeed, it could have been Vardy himself talking about the route he and Austin had taken. Austin had also started out in non-league before getting his break at Swindon, then moving on to Burnley and Queens Park Rangers. One big difference was that Austin arrived in the big league much earlier than Jamie – there is a four-year age gap between the duo, which makes Jamie's rise more remarkable and newsworthy. Fame should have passed him by – yet here he was, at twenty-eight years of age, usually the time when elite footballers have notched fifty caps or more, preparing for his debut. As the Hollywood scriptwriters kept telling us, Vardy's was some story: a real, one-off, rags-to-riches, obscurity-to-fame saga, worthy of the big screen.

A couple of days later Vardy and the England boys were training in front of the press and selected lucky supporters. The sun was shining and the boys were clearly happy and in good condition. Afterwards, Vardy signed autographs for invited guests and winners of England supporters' club competitions. Charlie Austin had been the first of the three newcomers to the squad to talk to the press and now it was Jamie's turn to face the spotlight. Naturally, many questions centred on his meteoric rise from nowhere to playing for England, and he admitted he had to keep pinching himself to check that it was happening; that he wasn't just dreaming.

Jamie was humble but determined as he explained that what had happened to him was a shock, but that he would give everything to keep the dream going. He said, 'It's a massive opportunity; I never thought it would happen. I've just got to take it in my stride and show what I can do. The lads have made me feel really welcome, as well as the gaffer, and it's an experience I'm never going to forget. When I was at Fleetwood I wouldn't have imagined I was signing for Leicester City, either. Every day I've had to pinch myself from where I've come from and to where I am now, and this is just the next step as well, which is even bigger. I'll be giving it my all. I want to show exactly what I can do and hopefully it's enough to get brought into the squad next time as well.'

He hoped he would get the chance to show his worth as the squad shut up shop a couple of days later and boarded a plane for Dublin. They were scheduled to meet the Ireland team at the Aviva Stadium, in front of a 51,000-capacity crowd on Sunday, 7 June. It was a momentous occasion for Vardy when Hodgson brought him on as a second-half substitute. But the result was a bit of a let-down – as the teams fought out a 0–0 stalemate. It meant England continued their nine-game unbeaten run but that Jamie had not grabbed the goal he would have loved to have nicked on his debut. But it was hardly his fault – the match was played at a pedestrian pace and neither side looked likely, or even keen, to score.

The Daily Telegraph summed it up with the rhetorical 'The worst England game in living memory' but added what we were all feeling in Fleet Street and across the nation, saying, 'However there was *one* redeeming factor for the game. Today will be remembered fondly by one man, and one man only – Jamie Vardy. The Leicester City striker made his England debut three years after representing non-league Fleetwood Town.' And so say all of us. Football fans up and down the country would agree with that sentiment.

Vardy made his debut on seventy-four minutes, replacing skipper Wayne Rooney. But he had little time and little chance to make an impact. He didn't have a single effort but, then again, neither did his colleagues in those disappointing final sixteen minutes of the game. But he was still grateful that he had been given the chance to earn his first cap – and hoped there would be more chances to shine in future games. 'I'm obviously over the moon. It literally is what dreams are made of,' Vardy told TheFA.com. 'Coming on for Wayne as well, I just thought I'd go out there, enjoy myself and try to show what I can do. I had a little chat with the gaffer beforehand – it was literally just do what I've been doing at club level and bring it on to the field to try and get the victory that we wanted. It was a strange game but it still keeps us unbeaten since the World Cup.'

Jamie said his aim was now to build on this debut and, hopefully, get another cap in the next imminent game, away in Slovenia. He added, 'We've got another week's training now and we will be preparing for the next game. So hopefully we can pick up a win over in Slovenia. I'll be going home, pinching myself and absolutely relaxing before we meet up again. I'll be doing everything I can, all I can do is give a hundred per cent in training and, if it catches the gaffer's eye and he give me that chance, then it's credit to the way I've trained. Training with the best players in England can only help me.'

At a subsequent press conference he elaborated upon his feelings, recalling a much more humbling time when he was a substitute: 'I remember the first time I was on the bench for Stocksbridge. It was Cammell Laird away, down on Liverpool docks. A few of the locals put the coach windows through. I couldn't tell you what with – we just got back to the coach and the windows were gone through.'

He was asked if he would agree he had come a long way as a footballer since then. He replied, 'Yeah, definitely. Jamie Vardy – England international? It does sound all right. I will be pinching myself later when I get home.'

And he stressed he would not be satisfied until he had performed for England as he knew he could, even though it had been a great thrill to even come on from the bench in Dublin, 'I was obviously over the moon that I had been selected to come on and as Wayne was coming off he said, "Good luck, just do what you do." I got told with Phil Jagielka after fifty-five minutes to go and warm up because we were going to be the next two substitutions. So I had the chance to get ready for it that way and come onto the pitch. It was a brilliant feeling. The emotion of the moment was a mixture of everything, but as soon as you take that step over the line that's when you have to get your professional head on and try to do the job.

'It was just to go on the pitch and do exactly what I've been doing to get the call-up in the first place, what I do at club level. There's no chance of anyone forgetting their England debut. My fiancée came over for the game and one of our friends came with her to keep her company. I've kept my shirt and the boys have signed it for me, which is an added bonus. I hope I've done enough to be involved [against Slovenia] and, if not, then I'll be trying extra hard this week to make sure that I have.'

On paper at least, the Slovenia match would be a tough examination of England's credentials. They were joint second in the group behind England – and had won both their home games with no goals conceded. It was a match England would win by 3–2 but it was a long journey with little end result for Jamie. He travelled as part of the squad but was not called on in a game, which saw Hodgson revert to his traditional conservatism, sticking with his usual roster of players both in his starting line-up and those he brought on from the bench. Rooney started up front with Raheem Sterling and Andros Townsend in support and the only forward change late in the game would be the introduction of Theo Walcott for Townsend. New charges Vardy and Austin were left unused and kicking their heels on the bench.

I was told that at least they had more experience of travelling with the squad and feeling part of it, but it would hardly have hurt to introduce one or both to add a bit more zest to England's game. Hodgson argued that the result was the key, and that is true. He picked up another three points on the way to France and his team had triumphed in a country where it was not easy to come away with a victory. But my thinking was that, okay, Vardy and Austin had been made to feel part of the group, but wouldn't it have been as well to give them both experience of what it is like to play for England in a competitive match?

Jamie had come on in the match in Dublin, but that had been a Sunday walk in the park with no ambition from either side. He would have benefited from wearing an England shirt in a game that counted, even if he had to come on as sub again. As for Austin, he could feel rightly aggrieved that his sum total of minutes since his call-up was absolutely nil. He had travelled long and far and returned home with no experience under his belt for his country. It was a shame – and also a reflection of how Hodgson tended to revert to his cautious type when the odds were great. If he was to do that during Euro 2016, England would likely be as disappointing and unadventurous as they were at the 2012 World Cup in Brazil, and that was something no England fan would like to witness. It would also lead to the end of Hodgson's four-year reign.

The manager was lucky that Rooney came to his rescue in Slovenia, grabbing the winner four minutes from time when it had looked as if Hodgson's innate caution had left them settling for the draw. Many pundits, including myself, had argued for the inclusion of Vardy at the expense of Sterling, who had seemed out of sorts in Dublin and who had his contract wrangle at Liverpool. Vardy would have added an edge that might have made the victory both more comfortable and more emphatic. He is not a player who sits on the peripheral: like Rooney, he demands to be part of the action and goes looking for the ball. But Hodgson stuck with Sterling and felt he had been justified after Rooney dug him out of a hole, saying, 'Wayne Rooney's performance said a lot about him as a man. He took a nasty blow from an elbow that could have decked many a player and could have caused him to lose his discipline, but he was up to concentrate on his job and his role in the team. One or two chances had gone begging but he got the chance for the winner and put it away with aplomb. It shows we can rely on that man. I would have liked him to have got a hat-trick so all the talk about the record [England all-time goals record] could have gone away.'

The squad returned home and Vardy at least had his first England cap to show for his efforts and time. He now had to show Hodgson he was worth another look as the England manager was not yet entirely convinced. Of course, Vardy now hit top form in the Premier League for Leicester and Hodgson was left with little choice but to pick him again for the Euro 2016 double-header qualifiers against San Marino away and Switzerland at home. Vardy was one of five forwards named in the twenty-three-man squad for the two games along with Rooney, Harry Kane, Walcott and Sterling.

Hodgson told the press, 'On this occasion we are obviously missing some players from the June matches. However, this is compensated by the fact we have players who weren't available over the summer. Jonjo Shelvey gets another chance, as he's been very impressive since the start of the season, whilst Ryan Mason has been unlucky with us – he picked up an injury the last time he was in the England squad. This latest squad shows we're working with a good number of players with a claim to be England regulars and secure a place in Euro 2016. Before that there are two matches we must focus on. The players must keep going, play well and look to win every match. I don't want any let-up and we want to win both these games.'

The pressure was on for Vardy – he would have to play well to keep his place in the squad, but, of course, to play well he would have to be chosen to play in the first place! It was back to St George's Park for more training sessions and one-to-one talks on 1 September 2015. Vardy worked hard to catch Hodgson and his backroom staff's eye, running at pace, beating defenders and scoring goals in key practice games. Three days later his efforts and persistence paid off, as Hodgson named him as one of three certain to start in San Marino, along with fellow squad battlers Jonjo Shelvey and John Stones. Jamie and Jonjo would be making their first starts for their country and both were looking forward with relish to the experience; both were also keen to leave a lasting impression by performing to the top of their ability.

Boss Hodgson also admitted that he too was excited by the prospect of seeing how the trio did in a competitive match. He told reporters, 'I don't really like to give the team out before the game, but there are some players that have invoked a lot of interest and speculation. So I can say that Jonjo Shelvey, who has had a brilliant start to the season with Swansea, will start the game as will John Stones and Jamie Vardy.

'John has done exceptionally well. It's a fact of life that the transfer window brings about speculation, but since he's been with us there's no question whatsoever: he is motivated to play. When Jonjo got his cap before, he was in a good period of his career, but a lot's happened since then. He's left Liverpool and joined Swansea, he's improved while he has been there, so I don't think it's so unusual that it's taken him a while to reach the level that we always thought he could reach.

'And you must remember that he's still only twenty-two; he's a very experienced twenty-two but he is only twenty-two and he's got every reason to look forward to a long England career if he can keep up the sort of form that he's shown at the opening of this season.'

Of Vardy, Roy also spoke in glowing terms, saying he had earned his chance because of his consistent displays for Leicester and his ever-growing reputation as a deadly goalscorer. Others were just as convinced that Vardy would do the business if given a run-out. Former Leicester ace

Bruno Berner, who played for Switzerland during his career, told the *Leicester Mercury* that Jamie would be a definite asset for England, saying, 'When you have a striker with his quality, pace and potential to cause you problems, it is something every manager would like to have in their attack. For a defender it must be horrible to play against him because you never know where he is. You have to check your shoulder all the time. The pace he has when he runs the channels, he could open up any back four or three with those runs in behind the defence. A lot of players these days want the ball to feet. He loves to run off defenders and he brings a great quality to England's game.'

And stats king Russell Cane, of fantasy football's Oulala Games, highlighted just why Vardy should start ahead of even Rooney in the upcoming qualifiers. He outlines the reasons why on the website talkingbaws.com, saying, 'In reality, Kane, Walcott and Vardy are all vying for one spot in the starting line-up, alongside Rooney. And it's Kane who is expected to line up with Rooney, despite his uninspiring start to the season. Stats released by Opta-powered fantasy football game www.oulala. com show that Vardy has not only scored more goals on his own than Rooney, Kane and Walcott have between them, but he also leads the other three for shot accuracy too. Fifty-seven per cent of the Leicester forward's shots have been on target this season. In contrast, Rooney has had an accuracy of just 43 per cent. Kane has hit only 38 per cent of his shots on target, with Walcott just 33 per cent. Boasting far superior attacking figures, Vardy should walk straight into the starting line-up against San

Marino on Saturday; however, it's unlikely, despite Kane and Walcott's poor starts to the season. Is a game against San Marino just what Kane needs to get his season up and running or is it the perfect opportunity to give the in-form Vardy the start that he deserves?'

In the event, Vardy did get the nod in San Marino, lining up alongside Rooney. Then, on the hour mark, Jamie worked with a new partner upfront when Kane replaced the captain. England ran out easy 6–0 winners but it was a disappointing night for Jamie. He never really got into the action and failed also to get on the scoresheet. *The Sun* pointed out that he had not been overloaded with assists to help him grab a confidence-boosting goal, adding, 'Starting Jamie Vardy was a bit of a surprise and the Leicester striker will need another eye-catching season to stay in Hodgson's plans. He would have loved a few more chances to open his England account on his first start.'

Some pundits felt he had been hit by first-cap nerves, but he rarely suffers from those. I felt it was more a case of not acclimatising to international football in the ninety minutes. Maybe he even tried too hard, given the pressure he was under to hit the ground running, with his fellow strikers all vying for the one spot next to Rooney. Some players take time to adjust to the international arena and I believe Jamie is one of them. It would help if he knew he was going to get a run to prove himself, rather than simply a one-off, but Roy Hodgson has his favourites and his own masterplan.

Jamie was pleased to win his first full cap but knew himself that he could have done better, could do better if he got the chance. And let's not forget that he did set up substitute Theo Walcott for a goal. But he was dropped to the bench for the next match against Switzerland and did not even get onto the pitch as a substitute. At least he had been part of the team that had rubber-stamped England's passport to Euro 2016; that 6–0 win in San Marino meant they had qualified with games to spare.

It would have done Vardy's confidence good if Hodgson had called on him for the Wembley clash with the Swiss. But, even if he had scored or played a belter, he would not have hogged the headlines. The 2–0 win included a goal from Rooney and it was his fiftieth for his country, which meant he had become England's all-time top scorer. It also meant, of course, that the headline writers and match reporters didn't need to worry about the angle they would take for the morning papers. Rooney had earned his right to be the main man.

My good friend Charlie Wyett summed it up best in *The Sun*, saying, 'The floodlights at Wembley are pretty decent. Yet at 9.25 p.m. last night, the light at the national stadium was boosted by 30,000 camera phones frantically trying to capture a moment of footballing history.

'Everyone here, including the Beckhams, had come to see Wayne Rooney become the first man to score 50 goals for England.

'They got their wish, all right.

It went on to add: 'Having equalled Bobby Charlton's record with a penalty against San Marino on Saturday, Rooney delivered probably the finest spot-kick of his career into the top left-hand corner.

'No goalkeeper in the world would have saved it.

'And no England striker for a very long time will get anywhere near his remarkable record.'

Rooney said he was overwhelmed by the moment, telling ITV Sport: 'To be the country's all-time leading goalscorer before the age of thirty is not something I could ever have dreamed of and I'm extremely proud tonight. I was a bit emotional out there and it's something to be extremely proud of. I'm happy it's done and hopefully I can kick on from here and concentrate on the team and our success in the future. I knew myself it was a big moment for me and I just picked my corner and put my boot through it to get as much power as possible and make it hard for the keeper. He got a touch but thankfully it had too much power. I went through a spell around 2008 when I didn't score for two years for England, and since Roy's [manager Hodgson] come in I've scored a lot of goals and I'm grateful to Roy for letting me play with the freedom that I enjoy.'

Rooney deserved the glory; his fifty-goal achievement is unlikely to be broken any time soon. Maybe Harry Kane will do it one day. He has age on his side, whereas Jamie Vardy was twenty-eight when Wayne broke the record and is limited to likely appearances given his age. But while Rooney won all the plaudits his performance overall was still not the same as that of the *twenty*-year-old Wayne, who used to terrorise international defences. He was in the team because of his record and because he was the captain – when there was actually a very good argument that the main strikers versus the Swiss should have been Vardy and Kane.

That was a view shared by many pundits, players, managers and fans. One former Leicester star, who was at the club when Jamie first arrived, led the calls for him to be his country's main man. Martyn Waghorn, now with Glasgow Rangers but who played upfront with Vardy for the Foxes, told the *Daily Record*: 'I don't see why Jamie shouldn't be first pick. Him and Harry Kane are the two best English strikers in the league right now. There are bigger names with more experience – Sturridge, Danny Welbeck, Rooney – but they're two young hungry players who want to work hard. Going into France you need energy and character as well as quality. As an England fan I'd be happy to see Jamie in the team.'

Five days after the disappointment of not being picked against the Swiss, Vardy was back scoring for Leicester, his late winner earning the points for the Foxes at Sunderland. It showed he could be relied upon to find the net when his place was guaranteed in a settled side. Now he would have to wait another month to see if Hodgson had kept faith with him for the next two European qualifiers, the final ones on the road to France the following summer.

Hodgson praised Vardy and the other newcomers for the part they had played in transforming England's fortunes after the depressing debacle in Brazil. He quite correctly said that the new boys had injected pace and hope into the team after England had looked so ineffective and slow in the World Cup.

But would he keep faith with Vardy for the final two qualifiers and the friendlies against Spain and France? If he did, that would surely mean the Leicester man was bang on target for a place in the final cut for France 2016.

CHAPTER TWELVE

DREAMING
OF FRANCE

When Roy Hodgson announced his England squad for the final Euro 2016 qualifiers Jamie Vardy was a little apprehensive. Never one to suffer from severe bad nerves or to fret too much about a future he could not control, Vardy nonetheless could be forgiven for wondering if his name would be among the chosen ones. He had not set the world alight in his previous outings, but he had shown the England boss he possessed the speed and quickness of mind to make an impact. At this stage of the international season, Hodgson was weighing up the pros and cons of all his players and wondering how they might fit into the overall jigsaw for France, if selected. As we have already suggested, Hodgson is an essentially conservative football head coach; he likes to stick with those he has tried and trusted. And Jamie's problem would remain the same throughout what was likely to be the final year of Roy's tenure.

Three of the four likely forwards for the championships would be Rooney, Kane and Sturridge, the last of these if fit. The fourth looked like being a straight choice between Vardy, Welbeck and Andy Carroll. The last two had suffered major injury problems during the season but the fact was this: Welbeck had long been a personal favourite of Hodgson and was the man most likely to get the vote unless he was injured. The England manager preferred the Arsenal man's business and willingness to get back and graft in defence, which was not always known to be one of Jamie's strengths in the game. But my preference would always be Vardy, even if only for the possibilities of his impact as a late sub in a game against tiring opposition legs. For all Danny's talent in helping out the midfield and defence, Vardy had one very big advantage: as this book went to the printers he was the third-highest scorer in English football, whereas Welbeck had never been a prolific goalscorer at club level.

It was surely a fair argument that Vardy should be chosen among the four *forwards* for that asset alone. He was a striker of goals, unlike Welbeck. And surely the central defensive midfielder and the four defenders should be talented enough to look after the shop at the back without having to rely on a striker to chip in. But Hodgson's instinctive conservatism would suggest to me that Welbeck could be alongside Vardy in the race for a place on the plane to France; at least that appears to be the case at the time of writing.

But two months is a long time in football – a lot can happen and, although of course Jamie would never wish ill fortune on anyone, should Welbeck 'break down' or become injured again, the Leicester man would surely at last be certain of his place. That is also assuming that Hodgson would choose him over the bull-in-a-china shop approach of Carroll, and that he would not decide that Theo Walcott was a striker, rather than an attacking midfielder.

There was much to be decided and much to be debated, but at least Jamie would be retained by the manager for those final two qualifiers, at home against Estonia and away in Lithuania. The FA announced the squad with the news that Hodgson had brought in Liverpool's Danny Ings as one of the strikers and *had* put Walcott into the group as part of a five-man club, which did still include Vardy. Ings would not be a threat to Vardy for France 2016 because a subsequent serious injury would rule him out altogether, but it was a worry that Walcott was now being viewed as a striker, and the five also still did not include the injury-prone Sturridge and Carroll. The chosen five for the two qualifiers were Rooney, Ings, Kane, Walcott and Vardy – and the FA presented the news in this way: 'England captain Wayne Rooney, who became the nation's top scorer with his 50th strike against Switzerland, is in along with Harry Kane, who scored the opener in that match. Theo Walcott, scorer of a quick-fire brace in San Marino, and Jamie Vardy are also part of Hodgson's strike-force. Having confirmed their place at the European Championship Finals earlier this month, Hodgson's side can now start to plan for next summer.'

Jamie spoke to the FA's website before the match, explaining that he took nothing for granted and that it had been down to hard work that he was even involved in the squad at the age of twenty-eight. He went on to say, 'Probably not until the first time I was called up, did I think I'd play for England. Obviously at every stage I've stepped up I wasn't expecting it to happen, but it did and I made sure I worked hard to keep there. And the steps have just kept coming and I need to keep that going. The secret is just lots and lots of hard work and the motivation that this is exactly what I want to be doing. As long as I put the work in all the way to the training field, or even if it's just in the back garden at home, it needs to be done to make sure you better yourself and you can make that transition and the step up.'

It was typical of the boy's down-to-earth approach and attitude to being the best that he could possibly be. He had come through the hard way and grafted to make each step count as he moved from non-league to the international arena. And he certainly wasn't taking anything for granted – he never had, so why start now? He knew more than anyone that only top-class displays would earn him a much coveted place in the squad for France. As he put it, 'It's another step up from what I've been doing. For anyone who plays for England it's an absolute honour. It's as simple as that. Putting the shirt on knowing that you are playing for your country, especially with the hard work I have had to get there, it's an unbelievable feeling. But as soon as I step over the white line it is simply another match.

'No one can take their place for granted. It's all up to me. If I want to be in that squad I've got to keep banging in the goals. I need to make sure I stay in the manager's plans, and if I've done that come summer we'll see.'

Walcott would get the nod above Vardy to start the match against Estonia and the *Sporting Life*'s betting odds suggested another way to solve the problem of Vardy or Walcott to start for the nation, saying, 'England's attack is likely to feature Theo Walcott, with Jamie Vardy possibly a more likely partner than Harry Kane, whose England career has so far blossomed from the bench. Vardy has made an undoubtedly fine start to the season in the Premier League, where he has seven goals in eight games, and, with Walcott, could be part of a lightning-fast pairing that would frighten many a defence. Vardy (at 100/30) and Walcott (4/1) are tempting bets to find the net first, but with question marks over England's starting eleven, it's a bit too much of a guess.'

The idea of 'a lightning-fast pairing' was one that would whet the appetite, for sure, although it was by no means the option Hodgson had so far shown any sign of favouring. Against Estonia, it would be one or the other, with Jamie earning another cap only seven minutes from the end, when he replaced Theo. It wasn't long to leave an imprint, but he did just that by setting up Sterling for the second goal in a 2–0 triumph for the hosts. It was an unselfish piece of play, as his speed took him clear of the visiting defence – he could have taken a shot himself, but selflessly stroked the ball across for Sterling's simple tap-in.

Two minutes were added on and another newcomer, Dele Alli, tried to set up Vardy as Jamie had done so with Sterling, but the attempted pass into his path was cleared by a determined Estonia defender. Still, it had been a very good night's work for Vardy considering the limited amount of time he had available to make any sort of impact.

'George', a contributor to the excellent fans' website, footballfan.zone, made the point that Vardy had maybe given Hodgson something to ponder upfront, because he was a different entity from the much-vaunted Rooney and Kane, and Vardy was another option, with his pace and intelligence, particularly with his tee-up for Sterling's goal, adding, 'It was a moment of maturity for the Leicester front man who could've easily decided to have a shot on goal but chose the right option in putting a ball on a plate for Sterling. Kane and Rooney are slightly similar, with the pair enjoying the ball at their feet but Vardy will have every chance of winning a place in Hodgson's Euro 2016 squad, especially if he keeps up his form for the Foxes. England are well stocked upfront with Rooney, Kane, Sturridge, Walcott and even Welbeck, so these impressive cameo appearances will no doubt do his cause the world of good.'

This was an excellent summary of the situation that Vardy found himself in as he now prepared for the second match of the October qualifiers, away in Lithuania. It was yet another win on the board for England as they came away with a 3–0 result, completing a perfect campaign. Sure, the opposition – apart from the Swiss – was of a standard they would not expect to lose to, or even draw to, but, as the saying goes, you can only beat what is put in front of you. And England under Hodgson in these Euro qualifiers had done just that. Whether it would be enough to even reach the quarter-finals in France, when the opposition were of a different league, was open to debate. Goals from Ross Barkley and Alex Oxlade-Chamberlain, and an own goal, sealed the victory. Vardy got a little more time to express himself than he had against Estonia, as Hodgson put him on from the start, as a partner for Harry Kane.

Again, he found it hard to stake a claim for a guaranteed starting place, and only entered the stats books by virtue of a booking for rushing forward from a defensive wall late on in the game. Kane probably put in a better performance and would have left the stadium as the more satisfied of the two. It was ten wins out of ten for England in qualifying, and Hodgson could not contain his delight, telling reporters, 'This is an achievement. I'm very proud of the players' performances. I thought it was excellent, in the first half especially. There was a lot of hard work put in, the quality of play was good and ten wins out of ten is very satisfying – we've got to take a lot of pride in that.

'I can't fault anyone tonight – a good performance, dominant and a nice way to end the qualifying campaign. It would have been a surprise if we had not qualified. But the upcoming friendlies are better, stronger sides. We'll see how we deal with that.'

The *Daily Mirror* complimented Vardy on his 'raw pace' that troubled the Lithuanian backline while *The Sun* also liked his speed of thought and strength on the ball. The latter is something that is not always commented on, yet, usually, Jamie's speed and knack of scoring after he has burst free of a central defender is the main talking point. But he is incredibly strong, and rarely loses control of the ball in a one-on-one confrontation. His control is good and he often brushes off the challenge of the biggest centre-backs while playing in the Premier League.

It is another facet of his talent – and one that should be taken into account by Hodgson if he is considering going for Vardy or Andy Carroll as a wildcard for Euro 2016. He's not as big as Carroll, but Vardy is just as determined and just as much a battler when the ball comes loose. Carroll's main advantage, of course, is his power in the air, but is that enough in the modern game? Wouldn't big defenders like Chris Smalling and Gary Cahill be able to pose that threat in the opposition box from corners? Vardy is faster than Carroll and just as tough; he also scores many more goals on the ground.

Jamie was called up again when Hodgson chose his squad for the two tough-looking friendly games against Spain and France. It was a tonic for the player that he made the squad – friendlies they may have been advertised as, but there was no doubt in the boss's mind that these two fixtures would provide a sterner yardstick to his team's progress. Ten victories out of ten against modest rivals in the qualifiers would count for little against two of the world's best international teams – and it was good news for Vardy that he continued to feature in Roy's plans.

The extra boost for Vardy was that he was one of only three strikers chosen by Hodgson for the double-header, along with Rooney and Kane. And Roy even used his press conference to publicly compliment the Leicester striker on his progress, admitting he had been 'pleasantly surprised' by his quality and adding that he was 'very useful' to have around. Roy told the press, 'I would be lying if I didn't say I was surprised, pleasantly surprised. When we selected him, I don't think there were a lot of people in the room saying, "Fantastic – that is a great idea as Jamie Vardy is the obvious man." And now you are. That is all credit to him. He has proved himself.

'He wasn't actually playing as a one hundred per cent regular for Leicester not so long back. He had some spells on the bench; now he is their main man; he is the top goalscorer in the League and has got a record at his fingertips, which he could at least equal with Van Nistelrooy, so that is all credit to him. All I can hope for is that he continues. He will, I'm sure. There's no doubt the qualities he has as a football player are very useful. They may be useful qualities for an international team.'

It was sweet music to the ears of Jamie and all his supporters. But then, just as he seemed set to start against Spain in his preferred central striking role, fate struck him a cruel blow. He got a knock in the Premier League win over Watford, which meant he missed out on the big match in Spain. Hodgson told reporters that it was a blow, saying, 'Jamie is the only injury concern but if we can spare as many players from playing in both games [it] will be good for us. It's very unlikely he'll be fit. We're hoping Jamie will recover and be able to play in the second game [against France at Wembley]. We've got lots of players and we will try and rotate them through the two games and make changes, so it's unlikely players will start both games.'

England skipper Rooney also accepted it was a disappointment for Jamie – and England – while adding it was a chance for Kane to shine, saying, 'It's a shame that Jamie picked up an injury because it was a big chance for him in these two games. But it's not just Jamie: Harry Kane has come into a good period of form and scoring for Tottenham. It's a good challenge for us all and hopefully we can show what we can do.'

In the event, Vardy was probably not gutted he missed the game in Alicante! England were given a footballing lesson by a country who have stars galore and know exactly how the game should be played. They monopolised possession to such an extent that the England players were exhausted by full-time after a ninety-minute pain barrier that saw them lose 2–0, although it could have been a much heavier defeat by a fine team who could well win Euro 2016. Hodgson tried to put a brave face on it, saying, 'We played against a very good team. It was pretty much as we expected. For seventy minutes we held our own and were getting back into it possession-wise. But we can't say we were the better team. They were the better team and deserved to win it.'

He now had to raise the morale of his troops for the next game, against France at Wembley. Jamie would, again, miss out because of injury as England gave a much improved display, winning 2–0. This time the result really was of little significance as the French looked lacklustre and didn't give their hosts a real game. This was hardly surprising, given that they had been forced to turn out at Wembley by their country's FA chief, just four days after the horrors of the terrorist attacks in Paris that had left many of their fellow citizens dead. Suicide bombers had also tried to get into the Stade de France as France took on Germany in a 'friendly' match.

So all involved could sympathise with the French players at Wembley and accept that the result was not a true reflection of the two teams' relative abilities. Jamie Vardy had missed both friendlies but it was, in hindsight, arguably for the best. In Spain, England were humiliated and against France they won, but it was a match that should not have been played anyway, given the devastation of the visiting players.

At least Vardy had now gone some way to convincing Roy Hodgson that he was not out of place in the international game, as the England boss had admitted. Whether that would be enough to earn Jamie a place in the Euro 2016 squad remained to be seen. But he had done all he could to be there – and would continue to do so as he stormed to the top of the goals chart in the Premier League by the start of February 2016. He had four months to make Hodgson one hundred per cent sure he should take him to France, and he would work damned hard to do just that.

CHAPTER THIRTEEN

EURO EXPRESS

The talk as the new year of 2016 dawned at the King Power Stadium was not whether Leicester could keep Jamie Vardy and his partner-in-crime Riyad Mahrez at the club in the looming transfer window. Rather, it was whether they could maintain their brilliant form and propel the Foxes into the European Champions League by finishing in the top four come the end of May. The fans were confident that the duo would stay until at least the summer, as they surely owed the club some loyalty after Leicester had given them their big breaks and stood by them until both had started to show top form. No, the fans at the King Power had other things on their minds — particularly the likelihood of playing in Europe. It would be a great gift from Vardy to the supporters he adored — and it could even help persuade him to stay at the club and shelve the move to one of the so-called 'Big Four' that many pundits claimed was inevitable.

Certainly, making the Champions League would be the greatest achievement in the club's history. The story of Leicester City in major European competition would barely fill a couple of chapters of a book, let alone a full tome itself. They played in the European Cup Winners' Cup in 1961–2 and the UEFA Cup in 1997–8 and 2000–1. So to make the Champions League either at the end of the 2015–16 season, or the following campaign if the club built upon the success of Claudio Ranieri's first season at the King Power, would be a remarkable feat. And even entry into the Europa League would be going some, considering the club appeared to be definite candidates for relegation early in 2015.

Chelsea boss José Mourinho argued that it was impossible that the Foxes would *not* finish in at least the top six before the Blues met Leicester in December 2015. 'They are in such a position where only three things can happen to them,' Mourinho told a press conference. 'One, to be champions, which would be amazing. Another would be to finish top four, which would again be a super achievement, but very normal at this moment because of the difference of points is very big.

'The worst thing that can happen to them is to finish top six, which should be a phenomenal season too. At this moment I don't think they are thinking about relegation any more. They are not thinking about finishing in the top half as that is certain. So at this moment they have conditions to enjoy playing free of any pressure but keeping that ambition that leaves them in this fantastic position.'

It may, of course, have been Mourinho utilising his famed 'dark arts' to try to catch Ranieri and Leicester off guard and treat his own team too casually. If so, it failed spectacularly as the Foxes still triumphed and effectively ended the Portuguese man's reign at Stamford Bridge. No, it was more likely that he was speaking as he saw it and, by the start of the new year, Leicester were joint top of the Premier League with Arsenal, both on thirty-nine points, although the Gunners had a better goal difference by +3.

Many in the press predicted that Leicester *would* make Europe as 2016 loomed. Charlie Wyett of *The Sun* said they would do just that after they beat Chelsea in December 2015. Wyett said, 'At the start of the inaugural Premier League season in 1992–93, Norwich were relegation favourites. They won the opening game of that season, beating Arsenal 4–2 at Highbury despite trailing 2–0 at the break, and they would stun English football by staying at the top. Mike Walker's team led the Premier League for virtually the entire season – and it was only an outstanding display of counter-attacking football at Carrow Road on April 5, 1993, that helped Manchester United set up their first title success in 26 years thanks to a 3–1 win.

'Norwich finished third, behind Aston Villa, and only secured European football – which resulted in a famous UEFA Cup win over Bayern Munich – because Arsenal won both cups. For the first time since, Leicester are on a fantasy ride when most expected them to be fighting at the other end of the table.

'At the start of this season, on social media, I predicted that Leicester would struggle this season and that Claudio Ranieri was "a terrible" appointment. I am certainly happy to have been proven spectacularly wrong and have subsequently been battered on Twitter. I am certainly not complaining. Some Leicester fans mistakenly think I wanted them to struggle which could not be further from the truth. But like many of the club's supporters – and even players – I thought Ranieri was a poor choice.

'Yet another fantastic performance against Chelsea on Monday proved that Leicester are in no mood to give up their role as surprise challengers. Way back, 23 years ago, Norwich had Mark Robins scoring the goals. Now, it is Jamie Vardy at Leicester. It would be the greatest thing possible for the Premier League if Leicester won the title and I would love to see them do it. Even if they fall away, there is still no reason why they cannot finish in a Champions League spot.'

And Ranieri eventually admitted in December 2015 that he *did* expect to take the club into Europe after refusing to countenance the idea up until that point. The Italian had made a point of saying the target remained the same – forty points so that they would be safe from relegation. But, in a quieter moment, he said, 'I think what I achieved is good and I want to get back there [Europe]. To play in Europe or the Champions League is fantastic and I want to help my players achieve this goal. You have to be solid at the beginning and know each other very well and then we can go there. I came here because I want to stay here a long time.'

City legend Gary Lineker also believed they could qualify

for major European action for the first time since 2000. In November 2015 he told BBC Radio Leicester, 'We've got a really tough run of fixtures coming up. Realistically, if Leicester qualified for Europe that would be a fabulous achievement. We've seen a lot of sides have a blistering start to the season then falter. But, looking at Leicester, we've got a decent squad. We're not just a freak side that's having a good run. They have done it now since early April. That suggests there's a terrific spirit in the squad. They're very good on the counter; there's bags of pace. If they can keep key players fit they can qualify for Europe. The Champions League won't happen. But I think Europa League is not impossible.'

Gary also stressed that Vardy would be key to that aim of making Europe – but added that in no way would he complain if Jamie quit the club for a big-money move in the summer of 2016 if his goals had propelled the Foxes into Europe. He told the BBC, 'A lot depends on Jamie Vardy and the attitude of the club themselves. He's twenty-eight. Who wouldn't want a big move at that stage of your career? Not just a payday but a chance to win trophies. Unless Leicester go on to win the league! If he continues that form he'll attract the big clubs, and who would deny someone, realistically, a move to one of the big boys? I did myself. It would be remiss of me to say he should stay till the end of his career.'

Another former City employee also predicted they would hit Europe. Dave Bassett was manager when the club were relegated from the Premier League in 2001–2 before going into administration, then became director of football as they quickly returned to the top flight. At the end of 2015 he told *Mirror Sport*: 'They are an old steam train on the move and they are going to take some stopping. I think they can stay there. I see them getting into Europe minimum. They will qualify for the Europa League – they have the points in the bag. When I was there the club went into administration. But they have moved on and whilst you can criticise foreign owners, these guys who have taken over the club have made all the difference. Before Leicester couldn't do it but they are rich enough to do it and the backing is there. Like anything it has to be right at the top. These people have given the backbone for the club to be able to compete financially. Leicester are not paying peanuts to their players, they are paying good wages. This is down to the owners who have supported the club.'

And the owners of the club were certainly aiming high. When Leicester won promotion to the Premier League in May 2014, billionaire Thai owner Vichai Srivaddhanaprabha made it absolutely clear he expected a top-five finish within three years and said he would put his money where his mouth was to achieve that dream. He told reporters, 'It will take a huge amount of money, possibly 10 billion Thai Baht [£180 million] to get there. That doesn't put us off. I am asking for three years, and we'll be there. We won't take the huge leap to challenge the league's top five clubs immediately. Do we have a chance to beat them? Yes, we have, but I think we need to establish our foothold in the league first and then we think about our next step.'

It was solid, sound thinking from the boss. Get established

in the top flight and then push on for Europe when the foundations are in place: no point aiming high and falling down just as quickly. The Thai chairman was clearly a man with a plan and by 2016 he was well on the way to achieving his European ambitions at the King Power Stadium.

He was not just in it for the money – he didn't need the money. As with Roman Abramovich at Chelsea, football was a passion to him. He treated the club and players with proper respect and in turn was respected by them. In 2010, *The Sun* had reported on his probable buyout – and even then it was clear this was someone who would bring a strong management to Leicester. My colleague Graham Hill reported thus: 'Leicester are set to be taken over by one of Thailand's richest men. Vichai, 52, was in advanced talks with Foxes owner Milan Mandarić to buy a majority stake as City prepared for today's opener at Palace. He is worth around £133 million and runs a Far Eastern shopping empire through his business King Power Group. Mandarić, 71, said: "There's a possibility a deal could conclude next week but there's no guarantee. What's important, if this deal is done, is it being the right people for the club. They are very plausible as far as football and Leicester City is concerned. We don't want to bring in people who are just here financially."'

Mandarić had a deep knowledge and love of the game and here he was himself expounding the virtues of the new owner. So, when Vichai announced his three-year plan for Europe, the fans sensed anything would be possible with him at the helm.

Yet the Fleet Street pundits remained well and truly split down the middle on whether City could qualify for the Champions

League come January 2016, though most of those whom I spoke with believed they could certainly finish in the top six if Vardy and Mahrez kept up their phenomenal goalscoring feats. That would put them on course for a Europa League spot, which would still be a massive achievement, given they were on the brink of relegation a year earlier. Fans throughout the land also were of the opinion that City were on course for Europe – and not just Leicester fans. One football fan spoke for many when he said, 'I'm stumped as to why so many people don't believe Leicester can do it! They are top, they have a great squad and they have shown no signs of slowing down – they've been on a roll since April. As an Everton fan, it's the wrong blue team to pick up the trophy, but, after their efforts this term, my goodness they deserve it. I for one would be happy to see them go all the way. Best of luck, you Foxes!'

And another made the point that fans generally – apart from those of the usual top six suspects, of course – were hoping fervently that City could maintain their excellent form and qualify for Europe, saying, 'The entire country is behind Leicester.' The form of Vardy and the efforts of his teammates appealed to the romantic sensibilities of supporters of the beautiful game, and it was a definite breath of fresh air that the team had roared to the top of the league when no one had expected them to be there. Vardy and Leicester had brought a refreshing breath of fresh air to a Premier League that had been becoming rather stale, with a top four that picked itself season after season – Chelsea, Manchester City, Manchester United and Arsenal.

What's more, with Jamie Vardy in such fine form as 2016 dawned, it appeared ever more likely that Leicester could make it into European competition. The odds favoured such an achievement and were backed up by the fact that Vardy was, in goal terms, the best striker in England – and second best in the whole of Europe! *The Sun* summed up that situation with findings to back it up, saying, 'Jamie Vardy is the hottest striker in the Premier League by a country mile. This season the Leicester hero broke Ruud van Nistelrooy's Prem record by netting in 11 consecutive games. And the England star has rippled the net in an incredible 15 times in 16 league games.

'Out of Europe's top five leagues – England, Spain, Germany, Italy and France – he is the second-best striker. Pierre-Emerick Aubameyang is the most prolific forward on the continent. The Borussia Dortmund forward has scored an incredible 18 league goals this campaign for the German giants. Aubameyang, 26, has been sensational since joining the Bundesliga side from Saint-Etienne in 2013. The lightning-quick striker has rippled the net 37 times in 84 appearances and is helping second place Dortmund keep up with Bayern Munich, who are five points above them at the top of the table.'

And not only did many pundits and fans now dare to believe that Leicester could make Europe, but some argued that the Foxes had rescued the game by making a rush for the top – and a consequent European adventure – with their brand of high-energy football. Chief among these advocates was John Williams, a senior lecturer in the Department of Sociology at the University of Leicester.

He contended that, by breaking up the monopoly of the big clubs at the top of the Premier League, Claudio Ranieri and his team had saved football. At a time when there was constant talk of the eventual evolution of a European Super League, consisting of the biggest clubs on the Continent (Germany, Spain and Italy) as well as from England, the Foxes' success was 'a bulwark' against that plan.

The club had brought romance back into the game at a time when money and 'the brand' seemed to conquer all. Williams concluded a brilliant essay in some style, saying, 'In an era when money and TV executives rule, City's pre-eminence has highlighted the enduring importance of some of the historically key features of sport: that cash alone can't ensure success; that quality players can still be found at value in the lower leagues; that motivation and team spirit are crucial features of any top team; that decent people can win out in football management; and, crucially, that fans still matter . . . football itself actually owes Leicester City a huge debt of gratitude: for no less than challenging the absolute power of money and for keeping the romance and the uncertainty of the game alive.'

The message from fans, players, managers and academics was loud and clear: Leicester City's achievement in pushing for a European place in 2015–16 was in itself a fantastic tribute to Vardy, Ranieri and the rest of the gang, but it could also be a watershed in Premier League and potential European Super League history. Finally, after many years of hegemony by the biggest, richest clubs, their dominance was now being challenged. The likes of Leicester – and even Crystal Palace, who were also having a fine campaign under Alan Pardew – showed that there was still a say for the romantics, as well as for those who believed the beautiful game was more, much more, than a brand for those with the most money to make more money, that it was not simply a conduit for financial gain. Okay, Leicester were owned by a billionaire, but he had shown a love of the sport and backed it all up with his actions – he was not in it simply to turn a buck.

Vardy and Leicester were bucking the trend, proving there should always be a place at the top table for the little guy. Lecturer John Williams was absolutely correct in his measured analysis: indeed Leicester had helped save football from itself in 2015–16. The club had shown how a love of football, backed up by sound investments in players who had cost peanuts in the terms of the modern game (Vardy at £1 million from non-league and Mahrez at £750,000 from France's Ligue 2), could change things for the better. Good management and class on the pitch had seen City thrive. No wonder Vardy did not want to leave in the winter transfer window early in 2016. He could see that if he stayed he might well become a Leicester legend, that is if he helped the club achieve that European ambition by the end of the season in May, as well as making his own mark in Europe via the Euro 2016 finals with England the following month in France.

Quitting the King Power in January could have jeopardised all of those key ambitions in the life of Vardy, the man who had become a lethal weapon for club and country as 2016 dawned.

Playing football at the highest level – at the Euros with England

and in Europe with Leicester – would be a challenge he would relish. Those three occasions in which City had competed in major European competition had not ended in glory, but with Vardy and co. it could be a different story. They would surely have a chance of going further than before, especially if Ranieri could strengthen his squad with genuine quality. In the 1961–2 season the adventure had lasted for four matches – a preliminary game with Glenavon and a first round against Atlético Madrid in the European Cup Winners' Cup. Even back then, the Foxes had a team not to be scoffed at: in the first leg against Glenavon, the team read: Gordon Banks, Len Chalmers, Graham Cross, Richie Norman, Ian King, Colin Appleton, Ian White, Gordon Wills, Howard Riley, Jimmy Walsh and Ken Keyworth.

Banks was the best keeper in the world and remains one of the, if not *the*, best ever to this day. And in Jimmy Walsh the 1961 team had their very own Jamie Vardy – although Walsh was the pride of Scotland, not England! Walsh grabbed a brace in the 4–1 first leg win in Northern Ireland. Another Scot, Hugh McIlmoyle, scored in the return leg at Filbert Street to take Leicester through on a 7–2 aggregate.

Ken Keyworth was on target for City in their next challenge in the competition, a 1–1 draw with Spanish giants Atlético Madrid in the first leg of the next round at Filbert Street on 25 October 1961 in front of 25,000 fans. But the Foxes couldn't score in the return in Madrid on 15 November, and exited the tournament with a 2–0 loss in front of a crowd of 50,000.

It would be another thirty-five years before Leicester would again participate in major European competition – and once again Atlético would prove to be their nemesis. This time the clubs met in the UEFA Cup with Los Rojiblancos emerging winners by an aggregate score of 4–1. Foxes fans were still hopeful after the club lost 2–1 in Madrid but a 2–0 loss in the return wrecked the dream. However, there had been no disgrace in the defeat, as there was a massive inconsistency in the financial make-up of the teams – as *The Independent* pointed out in a match report from the first leg on 16 September 1997, 'Atlético Madrid, parading £51 million worth of talent, scored twice in three minutes to ensure that they take a slender advantage to Leicester for the second leg of their UEFA Cup first-round tie a fortnight hence. But the Coca-Cola Cup holders' £7.5 million line-up frightened them, defending Ian Marshall's goal until late in the game, and are by no means out of this one yet. Juninho, who grew in influence as Leicester tired, brought Atlético level with 21 minutes remaining. Christian Vieri settled the issue, at least for the night, by converting a strongly disputed penalty.'

The Leicester team that night read: Keller, Prior, Elliott, Walsh, Guppy, Kamark; Izzet, Lennon, Parker (Fenton, 71), Marshall (Claridge, 30; Campbell, 90), Heskey. Subs not used: Whitlow, Cottee, Savage, Andrews.

Two years later, City returned to UEFA Cup action against Red Star Belgrade of Yugoslavia but would again fall at the first hurdle. They drew 1–1 in the first leg at Filbert Street on 15 September 2000, with Gerry Taggart heading them level. But it had not been an easy night with the visitors bossing play. The only consolation would come in the form of the return leg being played at a neutral ground in Vienna because of the political and social unrest in Belgrade at the time.

Yet even that would prove little consolation, as Red Star won 3–1 at the home of Rapid Vienna to take the tie 4–2 on aggregate. Red Star had been miffed at the location – as UEFA had expected. 'To be honest, I don't think that Red Star will be overjoyed with this outcome, but after taking everything into consideration we do believe that Vienna is the right and proper choice of venue,' Mike Lee, UEFA'S director of communication, had said. 'But that is now the end of the matter. Red Star did not agree with Leicester's initial objection to the game being played in Belgrade but their appeal, after due consideration, was rejected by us.'

But Leicester manager Peter Taylor said, 'I am pleased the venue for the game has now been settled. Once Sunday's game is out of the way things will be clear and we can plan for the second leg.'

And club chairman John Elsom would outline his belief – much mistaken, as it transpired – that the neutral venue would be better for players and fans. He said, 'By moving this game to Vienna, all the concerns which my club's players will have had will have been removed. We are all very pleased with this outcome and I must thank UEFA for the way this whole matter has been handled.'

In the event, Leicester would lose 3–1 and their supporters would face a nightmare trip. The 2,000 fans came under attack from missiles outside the stadium and from flares thrown by imbeciles among the 8,000 Red Star followers inside the ground in a thoroughly depressing outing. In addition, Ade Akinbiyi and Andrew Impey were subjected to 'monkey chants'.

Muzzy Izzet had given the Foxes hope when he equalised, but the Yugoslavs triumphed and Leicester were out of major European competition early on yet again. Hopefully, if Vardy's goals fired them into Europe, the outcome would be more pleasing and more pleasant both on and off the pitch – for the team and for the loyal fans who continue to follow them through thick and thin. It is the least the supporters deserve after sticking with their team through the bad times that dogged them as they struggled to find consistency and stability off the pitch, with ownership issues over the past couple of decades. And Jamie Vardy was determined that they should have something to celebrate – both in the domestic arena and in Europe – after they had encouraged and backed him as he himself strove for consistency and form following his transfer from Fleetwood. He loved the Leicester fans and that feeling of admiration was mutual. Together, they had already achieved great things – and the fans hoped that would long continue.

CHAPTER FOURTEEN

JACK
THE LAD

There's been a tag that Jamie Vardy has been keen to get rid of as his career advanced so rapidly from non-league to potential international superstar during 2015 and 2016: 'troublemaker'. He would be the first to admit he has always been someone who plays with fire in his belly and who has an edge to his game. So did the likes of Roy Keane and Patrick Vieira, but while the indiscretions of these two were eventually viewed as a positive, in that they contributed to the players they became, Vardy's fire and passion have often been used as a stick with which to beat him.

Some of the journos in Fleet Street I spoke to about Jamie contended he 'had a bad attitude' and that he was 'not the sharpest knife in the drawer', while others said he was moulded from the streets and 'did not have the nous to walk away from trouble'. Some of them believed he was a fight waiting to happen, and that he would be a gamble in international football and even at one of the so-called 'Big Four' clubs, because he was a hothead; that he could not control his temper and would lose it in big games, thus costing his teams dearly, because they might end up playing with ten men.

There were also criticisms of his life off the pitch, with claims that he could be trouble on a night out, allegations drawn largely from an incident that occurred early in his career and another one at a casino in 2015.

But the overall stats and the facts do not support the general claims that Vardy is a troublemaker, and are even less indicative that he is some kind of yob to be steered clear of at all costs. My view is that he is now a settled guy who adores his fiancée Becky, and who enjoys a simple (if luxurious) lifestyle with his family. Sure, he had his problems growing up, and there were isolated difficult incidents later, but now, in 2016, he is on the straight and narrow. The fact is that he would certainly be bombed straight out of the England squad if he was such an unsavoury character as some in the press may try to portray him as. No way would Roy Hodgson, a genteel character, have a yob aboard his train.

And Vardy is certainly not in the league of, say, such firebrands as Chelsea's Diego Costa on the pitch. The latter is renowned as a player who seeks out confrontation, who thrives when he is in a pitch battle, whereas Vardy thrives most when he is racing away from a defender and scoring, rather than trying to wind his opponent up (as Costa enjoys doing).

Look at the last five years of Jamie's career and you will find
that he has only been sent off once, and that was when he
was playing for Fleetwood Town in 2011. Compare that with
Costa, who has been sent off seven times in his professional
career – and let's not forget that the Spanish player is a year
younger than Vardy. Costa's offences have included headbutting,
stamping and dissent.

For his part, Vardy, wearing number 33 on his shirt, was shown
the red card playing for Fleetwood against Kidderminster on
20 September 2011. He got his marching orders, along with
Harriers' Steve Guinan, on the half-hour mark when the score
was 0–0. Jamie was sent off for a bad tackle and Guinan also
had an early bath after throwing a punch. Luckily for Vardy, the
Cod Army still won – and at a canter, too, as they emerged 5–2
winners. Fleetwood's official website described the Vardy run-
in like this: 'Victory was marred by ugly scenes in the first half
when both teams came together after Town's Jamie Vardy had
committed a foul which resulted in a red card and a probable
three-match ban. Kidderminster's Steve Guinan joined him
after striking Town skipper, Jamie McGuire, as the game
threatened to lose control . . . Vardy went in heavily and sparked
an angry confrontation between both sets of players and the
two benches. It took some time for the referee to exert control
and his response was to red card both Vardy and Guinan.'

The Harriers' website also reported on the bust-up, criticising
Vardy but nonetheless calling him Fleetwood's 'consummate
goal-scorer', going on to say: 'The game erupted when
Fleetwood's James Vardy lunged with both feet at Vaughan and

clearly this challenge was going to result in a straight red card for the previously consummate Fleetwood goal-scorer. Incensed, Kyle Storer embarked upon petitioning the referee and Steve Guinan decided to take matters into his own hands by flailing his arms in the direction of Jamie McGuire. Both management teams then became embroiled in the highly unseemly fracas and inevitably Guinan was also shown a red card and booed off the pitch by the home crowd. Thereafter a semblance of order was regained.'

Harriers boss Steve Burr was full of praise for Fleetwood's conviction after the sending-off, saying, 'It all went wrong when we went down to ten men and they went down to ten men. They worked a lot harder than us. We were in control in the first half, then the incident where the two lads were sent off, and they were better than us in the second half.' So Vardy's dismissal served to gee up his teammates, although his boss Micky Mellon said he would prefer a quieter day next time Jamie played! Mellon, too, was involved in the altercations, with the *Fleetwood Weekly News* observing, 'The two managers had to be separated on the final whistle, with altercations continuing in the tunnel. But Mellon refused to let the ugly scenes mar an excellent night for his side, who are one of four teams tied on 20 points at non-league football's summit.'

Mellon was more interested in praising Vardy for his goalscoring exploits for Fleetwood than demonising him for his part in the Harriers' bust-up. He told BBC Radio Lancashire he was delighted with the goals Jamie was scoring and that the win over Kidderminster had made it fourteen goals scored in four games, which had enabled the Cod Army to move up to fourth in the Blue Square Bet Premier, continuing to say, 'At the end of the day, that's how you win games of football. But it's also great that the goals are getting shared around, and some we are scoring are top-drawer.' It meant Mellon's men had won six of their first ten games, and were already on course for a promotion campaign although he warned, 'We have achieved nothing except for another three points.' Yet, with Vardy on fire throughout the season, they would achieve something: promotion to the promised land of the Football League.

Vardy's fire is undoubtedly a result of the battle he had to make it in the game. In earlier chapters, we have dealt with his upbringing and battle to make the grade and how that moulded him into the man and the player he would become. It was never an easy ride and that is why Vardy is such a determined character; he developed into the aggressive, winner-takes-all sportsman he is because he fought every step of the way on the journey. Nothing came easy, nothing was put on a plate, he was not the product of a pampered academy with a big club. Fight, fight, fight – it's little wonder he can sometimes appear to thrive on the edge, but he has done well over the past couple of years also to learn when to back away when a decision is 50:50, or when dissent could get him dismissed.

Admittedly, he can still get in a tangle with rivals and pick up more than his fair share of yellow cards – more of that later in this chapter.

But, while our example of Diego Costa is that of a man who thrives on confrontation and winding up rivals to the point where they explode and get sent off (Arsenal's Gabriel for instance), I would argue that Vardy does not set out to get opposition players in trouble. He argues when he thinks he has been wronged, or when someone is trying to belittle him, or if he considers that a decision has incorrectly gone against the team – but he is no wind-up merchant à la Costa.

In his earlier non-league career, it's been suggested Jamie could be a bit wilder and less disciplined. Allen Bethel, chairman of Stocksbridge Steel, where Jamie ended up after being rejected by Sheffield Wednesday, called him 'a Jack the Lad'. Bethel said, 'We had some trouble with him, not trouble for me but trouble in the sense he was a bit of a boy, who got into trouble going into Sheffield on Saturday nights. He was a Jack the Lad but never rude to us. He did a few silly things on Saturday nights – a few people targeted him.'

It was while playing for Stocksbridge that he also, infamously, had to contend with wearing an electronic tag on his leg. Vardy took up the story of the 2007 incident while preparing with the England squad for the match against Ireland in Dublin in 2015. He told reporters he had been convicted of assault and was compelled to wear the tag for six months, saying, 'It was a hard time for me and my family. I had to be in the house from six at night to six in the morning. I wasn't able to do what any normal twenty-year-old would be doing. All my mates were out enjoying themselves and I was locked away in the house. Luckily, I had a big DVD collection!

'You could wear the tag like an ankle guard. Even if you got kicked, there was no way it was breaking. You could hit it with a hammer and it wasn't coming off. And, now I think about it, not being able to go out with my mates probably helped me in my football career.'

I admired the way Jamie spoke about the incident honestly, and even found a way to see how it could be a positive in his life, despite the problems it caused. Also, it was good to hear him admit he was 'not proud of what I did'. He took his punishment and moved on, still working hard at his football while trying to turn a coin in his factory job.

Allen Bethel also had a view on the incident that led to the tag, saying, 'Jamie did not start the fight – but he ended it.'

Vardy still managed to make headlines when he joined Halifax Town and then Fleetwood. During one match, play was held up when a pitch invader took centre stage – and it was Vardy who took it upon himself to sort out the problem. He earned the nickname 'The Cannon' after firing himself at the miscreant. Vardy added, 'A mad man got onto the pitch and, because of my size, I had to lead from the front and be aggressive. That's how I got my nickname.'

At Fleetwood, he remained the same committed, down-to-earth lad who 'needed keeping an eye on' but who, according to vice-chairman Phil Brown, was a winner from the outset, as he described: 'He was someone to keep an eye on. He knew how to enjoy himself, shall we say. When he was off the leash, he was someone who would find himself in a little bit of bother. He knew how to let his hair down but he never caused us any real problems.'

His former Leicester boss, Nigel Pearson, has the same view:

that Jamie is a man who would not let him down after he gambled on signing him, despite the problems he had encountered in a somewhat troubled past. Pearson was delighted when Jamie was called up for England and told reporters he would never want to change the player, that he 'had an awful lot of time for him . . . warts and all'.

Pearson said, 'It's quite an amazing turnaround. When you look at his career in its entirety, it's a good story, it's probably the type of story that hasn't happened in recent generations of players. Jamie's not as straightforward a character as you would probably think he is. He's had a few situations that he's had to deal with on and off the field. And, as most players do from time to time, he's suffered with confidence, which had coincided with other aspects he's had to deal with. But he's a likable lad. He's someone I have an awful lot of time for. I'm really pleased for him. I hope he's able to enjoy the experience. I'd never want Jamie Vardy to be anyone other than Jamie Vardy. Warts and all.'

Another professional who admired Vardy, and his determination and battling qualities to reach the top after a fight to get there, is former Hull City player Jimmy Bullard. He himself had made it from non-league and revealed that playing there had helped to build his character and strengthened his resolve to succeed – traits he also saw in Vardy and fellow non-leaguer-turned-England-star Chris Smalling. Bullard told the website squawka.com, as part of Ladbrokes Rugby's 'Who's Got the Balls' campaign, 'I'm a massive, massive fan of Vardy. If you've got pure pace these days, half a brain and half a good touch, you can make something of yourself. Pace is so important and he's just got blistering pace. He gets right on the shoulder and looks to get past him all the time. But he can also come and play to feet and that's what I like about him. He mixes it well but he's looking to get in behind at every opportunity.'

In 2015 Jamie was in the headlines again for the wrong reasons. It was alleged he had abused an Asian man at a casino late at night. A video showed him saying to the man, 'Yo Jap, walk on,' and he could be heard saying the word 'Jap' three times during a game of poker. Jamie immediately apologised for his actions, saying, 'I wholeheartedly apologise for any offence I've caused. It was a regrettable error in judgement I take full responsibility for and I accept my behaviour was not up to what's expected of me.'

A Leicester spokesman added, 'We expect the highest standards from our players on and off the pitch and for them to set an example as role models in our community. We have noted Jamie's apology and will begin a process of investigation into the incident imminently. There will be no further comment until this process has concluded.'

When the 'process' was concluded, City issued another statement, saying Vardy would be fined heavily and would attend a diversity-awareness training programme. The statement said, 'Leicester City Football Club has concluded its investigation into claims made against Jamie Vardy in the national media last weekend. Having established a full account of the incident in question and taken into consideration Jamie's prompt apology, the club has issued the player with a substantial fine and prescribed a programme of diversity awareness training.

Jamie has been reminded of his responsibilities to the club, his profession and the Leicester community. The fine will be donated to local charities. The club will make no further comment on the matter, which it now deems to be closed.'

Earlier, Foxes boss Claudio Ranieri had been asked at a press conference if Jamie would be sacked because of the incident. He said, 'No. It is not my matter, but he won't be. The situation is everything is okay, Jamie apologised to everyone, it was a mistake. The relationship is okay. We go on and forward. The club has said it is okay. James has apologised and for me it is okay.'

It had been a close call and a most unsavoury incident. Vardy's apology did seem sincere and he was, understandably, keen to move on and put the issue to bed – although that was not easy, as many commentators claimed he was a racist and should be sacked by Leicester. A few weeks later Vardy did an interview with Sky Sports and his regret and shame were apparent; he was sincere in his admission that he was wrong, out of order and that there would be no repeat. He told the TV channel's sports news HQ, 'I got into an altercation, which is not like me at all. It's definitely out of character and I regret it massively. I asked the club to get in touch with the lad and bring him into the training ground so I could apologise to him and talk things through. He was happy to come in and talk about what happened and we sorted it all out. After we had the meeting there were no hard feelings and I just want to move on from it now.'

It was a warning that the further up the ladder you got in

professional football, the more you are under the spotlight, and the more you were expected not only to behave but to set an example. Jamie Vardy was now at the top of his profession but, as I stated at the start of this chapter, his lifestyle is much more settled in 2016 and he is much more stable, happy and contented with his lot.

Of course, there were run-ins on the field, even during the most recent 2015–16 campaign. Vardy will never lose that spark, the edge that makes him a striker who never gives up and never gives in, whether it be chasing a ball that looks as if it is going out of play, or a back-pass to an opposition keeper that has gone astray. That is why he is such a dangerous striker: he is always alert, always awaiting an error or a chance to pounce. No sane defender would turn his back on him when he is nearby.

We have spoken of the differences between Vardy and Diego Costa, how the Brazilian-turned-Spaniard will deliberately wind up a rival to get him sent off, while Vardy is usually the confronted person rather than the confronter. Yet in the 2015–16 season Jamie and Diego would cross paths – and it told me just how tough the lad from Sheffield was, as he refused to be intimidated by Costa. Indeed, he gave as good as he got.

The duo squared up after a bad tackle by Vardy. Costa, as is his norm, put his face right into Vardy's. But while most players would have backed off and quivered – Costa is one of the most intimidating players, after all! – Jamie didn't give an inch. It was good to see Spain's adopted striker stood up to for once. Many fans agree that Costa is arguably the most provocative player in the Premier League but Jamie was not at all threatened or fearful of him. Who does not like to see the school bully brought down to size? The duo eventually backed away from each other, but it was noticeable that Costa did not try it on again with Jamie again that day.

It was the day when Jamie would be better remembered for a message left on the seat of every Leicester fan in the stadium. Before every home game the club left a cardboard clap-banner, which became known as 'clappers' as the season progressed, on every supporter's seat. These clappers made a real racket when they were used in unison and it was as if the fans were roaring their heroes on. At a cost of £12,000 per game – over £200,000 for the season – it was a nice move by the club's executives, and guaranteed that the team were always well backed by their fans.

Before the Chelsea match, Vardy's message and signatures appeared on the clappers. He thanked the fans for their fantastic support, saying, 'On behalf of the team I'd like to say a huge thank you for the magnificent support we've received this season. Hearing the roar of the crowd makes us believe that anything is possible and we hope you realise just how big a part you have to play.'

Leicester spokesman Anthony Herlihy said, 'Senior management at the club feel this helps create a very positive atmosphere at the stadium. It is quite an undertaking to place clappers on 30,000 seats but we think it is well worth it. The clappers allow the supporters to make a big difference on match day. They can all join in and make as much noise as they want to support their team.'

Former Foxes star Alan Birchenall, now club ambassador and stadium announcer, told the *Leicester Mercury*, 'The idea of giving the fans something to make a noise with is not new. But something special has happened with these clappers. They were a hit immediately with the kids and the mums but now the dads have joined in. When I go out onto the pitch before kick-off when the teams are in the tunnel, the sheer noise makes the hairs on the back of my neck stand up.'

And Carolyn Israel, MD of Clap-Banners Ltd, added, 'Clap-banners are made from specially developed, high-quality material that allows them to be used robustly by the fans as a hand-held clapper as well as a visual hand-held banner.'

Vardy's confrontation with Costa had shown that he would stand up to anyone who tried to bully him or push him around, but at the same time he was working hard to improve his disciplinary record. Ranieri had explained to all his players before the start of the season that yellow cards added up and suspensions could cost the team dearly in the long run. It was a message that all the Leicester boys took on board – they knew that indiscipline led to self-punishment, in that it meant missing matches and could even make it hard to get back in the side if your replacement did a good job while you were banned. Plus, there was the little matter of not wanting to let down your teammates because you had been unable to control your temper.

A yellow card for a rash tackle was one thing; however, a yellow card for dissent was quite another. And, by the start of February 2016, Vardy had picked up just five yellow cards for Leicester in twenty-five appearances. That is not a bad record given his competitive nature and his desire to win. The previous season, when Leicester had been battling relegation, he was booked six times and the campaign before that (2013–14) received nine bookings. So his ability to stay out of the referee's notebook seemed to be improving season by season.

Of course, being such a fiery player would mean that Vardy would inevitably have some run-ins with opposition stars – and, given his elevation to being one of England's top five strikers, those would generate headlines. For example, on 16 January 2016, Jamie had a bust-up with Aston Villa's Leandro Bacuna as the Foxes went back to the top of the Premier League with a 1–1 draw at Villa Park. *The Sun's* 'Goals' pullout featured a picture of the duo face to face with the headline, 'Come and have a go if you think you're Vard enough!' Tellingly, the picture showed Bacuna with his arms around Jamie's neck, with the accompanying words, 'Foxes and England striker Vardy was grabbed round the throat by the Villa full-back and the warring pair had to be pulled apart by team-mates.' Like Diego Costa, Bacuna was the aggressor and Jamie had stood up for himself. But his actions cost him a booking by referee Roger East in what had been a frenzied Midlands derby.

However, *The Sun* also paid tribute to the part Vardy had played in taking the Foxes back to the top for a fourth time in the season, saying, 'The Foxes, then bossed by Nigel Pearson, won seven of their last nine games to stay up – and that form has continued this season under Ranieri, with a big part played by Vardy. It is easy to see why the former non-league striker has got his success – 15 goals and an England call-up – as he puts in some serious yards. Even when it looks like a lost cause, he never gives up . . . it was not long until Vardy was causing more havoc for the Villa defence to deal with – eventually setting up the opening goal. He raced on to a long punt forward from Schmeichel that [Jores] Okore should have dealt with and produced a stunning lob. [Mark] Bunn backpedalled to claw the ball away and also blocked Okazaki's rebound, but technology gave ref Roger East the nod that the ball had crossed the line.'

That is a good summary of Vardy and the type of player he is: he never gives up and is a pest for defenders, who are always having to look over their shoulders to see where he is and what he is up to. He is a nightmare to play against – and sometimes can be a nightmare to come up against, as Costa and Bacuna would testify. That is the nature of Vardy the footballer – you take him as you find him, good and bad, a scorer of brilliant goals but whose very presence, ability to irritate opponents and refusal to be bullied can lead him into confrontations. Even when he was at Fleetwood, Jamie could find himself on the wrong end of inflamed passions as he recalled, 'In my year at Fleetwood, we played at Luton and that was just carnage. We were winning 1–0 at half-time, I'd dinked the keeper and obviously celebrated a bit madly. Their fans were rocking the tunnel and all their players were trying to get hold of one of our strikers. The police came into the dressing room and told us if we were going to start a riot they'd lock us up.'

He is honest enough to tell it straight about his game and how he has thrived from the bottom to the top in less than four years, saying, 'I'm just a pest. That's all I've ever been. I don't know how to play any different. There is no sitting off, I just go straight at them.' That is why defending against him is such an ordeal: because he never gives you a moment's peace or time to catch your breath. As with all fine players who have made it to the top with a reputation for fieriness – for instance Roy Keane, Alan Shearer and Wayne Rooney – it is that very fieriness that makes them the footballers they are. You take away the fire and you take away the passion and that unrelenting desire to win. Jamie Vardy may be criticised for being a hothead in some circles, but he has never denied what he is or where he has come from and how it has moulded him into the person and footballer he is.

Ruud van Nistelrooy, the man whose goals record he broke in 2015, had bust-ups with fellow players and even with his manager, Sir Alex Ferguson, and could be relied upon to wind up defenders who could not stop him. By 2016 Jamie Vardy was keen to improve as a player and a person – and he admitted there were episodes off the pitch that he very much regretted and would not let happen again. But he would never lose that passion, that will to win or that desire to be the best on the pitch. It was, after all, what had helped him secure the goals record that had made him globally famous in the first place.

CHAPTER FIFTEEN

LEAGUE OF HIS OWN

A big part of the Jamie Vardy rise to being a top-flight 'goal machine' lies in his development from non-league battler to Premier League star. It is the very fact that he spent time in non-league football and was plucked from its relative obscurity and given his chance in pro football that makes his story so heart-warming and such a rise of epic proportions. Jamie himself is the first to say it is indeed something of a fairy tale and that you couldn't pen a better script for a movie plot (as some have suggested his life story might even become, and, if so, that it could be a real cinema success).

And Jamie has also put his money where his mouth is by coming up with a plan to help others make the breakthrough as he himself did. In 2015 he announced he would set up his own academy to bring through players from non-league – with the basic premise being that he would put something back into the footballing arena that had given him a shop window from which to launch himself into the big(ger) time.

Jamie confirmed that the idea had germinated from a desire not to forget where he had come from – to give credit to his own footballing roots with a positive contribution. It would also show players that, even if they were initially rejected by professional clubs, it was not necessarily the end of the road. He himself, of course, had been turned away by Sheffield Wednesday as a youngster but had battled back and made it to the top. He had refused to give in and he now wanted the thousands of hopefuls who also suffered the same heartache at sixteen or eighteen to know that there could still be a future for them; that persistence and dedication were the key; that 'talent would out' if you kept working hard and knocking at the door of opportunity. He revealed that the academy would be known by the moniker 'V9' – a nod to his name and shirt number.

The plan had been taking shape for months and in November 2015 he revealed how it had come about and how he hoped it would develop. He said, 'I know there are players out there in a similar position to where I was, that just need an opportunity. More and more players are dropping out of the system early. For me, it was at Sheffield Wednesday when I was sixteen because they thought I was too small. I remember how that felt and it's difficult to come back from or even think about the professional game.

'I want to give people the shot I was given because there are some talented players in non-league. There are a lot of teams that won't take the gamble and probably will rather pay over the odds to get a player who has the experience but they might not do it either. With teams taking a risk on non-league players it will only benefit the game and make the English game altogether a lot better.

'I've thought for some time that something could be done about it and after several conversations with my agent, John Morris, and my fiancée, Becky, we decided to set up V9 to unearth talent and give those players a shot – hopefully at earning professional contracts but also to learn and understand what it takes to be a professional at the highest level.'

Jamie became non-league's first £1 million player when he signed for Leicester from Fleetwood in 2012. He said that the first influx of non-leaguers into V9 would begin in summer 2017 and that they would undergo a week of coaching that would enhance their technical, tactical, physical and psychological strengths and help them to develop. The coaching would be supervised by coaches with Premier League or Football League experience. As well as being coached to improve their play, the chosen ones would learn about other key aspects of pro football, including nutrition and sports psychology.

They would meet at a centre in England and be encouraged to believe in themselves. At the end of the week-long course the players would be handed a detailed file of information of their strengths and areas in which they could work on and improve – and, hopefully, make the transition from non-league to the professional arena as they took note and worked on their individual development dossiers.

Jamie said that around sixty players would be taken in at the academy, although many more are likely to apply. He had set up a website, v9academy.co.uk, so that the hopefuls could apply for a place on the course.

And Jamie's agent, John Morris, was just as enthusiastic about the academy and is determined to make it work. He said, 'For the players that show the aptitude to play in the Football League, we will work closely with them to make sure they are placed in the best football environment to go and fulfil their potential.

'We believe there are many more Jamie Vardys out there. The V9 Academy aims to find them.'

Morris wasn't simply playing lip service to his client's dream, either. The agent had already proved he believed in non-league players and that they could make the grade in the Football League. He had negotiated Vardy's move from Fleetwood to Leicester and two other notable transfers. In 2014 he took Joe Lolley from Kidderminster Harriers to Huddersfield Town for a fee said to be around £300,000. The right-winger-cum-striker was born in Redditch near Birmingham and worked under the auspices of City's academy until the age of sixteen. He was then released and joined Bromsgrove, but made a name for himself at Midland Combination side Littleton, scoring eighty-eight goals in just eighty-three games. At the same time, he studied for a sports-coaching degree at the University of Central Lancashire in Preston. Playing for the university, he went on to represent Great Britain at the World University Summer Games in Russia in the summer of 2013 – reaching the final before defeat to Russia.

It was on the tour that he made a link with Kidderminster, as their coach Steve Guinan also helped coach the GB team in Russia. Lolley signed a one-year contract at Kidderminster and was then snapped up by Huddersfield in the deal negotiated by John Morris. Huddersfield had great hopes for Lolley – and if anyone could help him develop from non-leaguer to pro star it was their manager, Mark Robins. Robins was the man who, according to folklore, saved Sir Alex Ferguson from the sack three years into his twenty-six-year Manchester United career – when he scored the winner in an FA Cup clash against Nottingham Forest in 1989. United went on to win the trophy and Fergie's years of glory began, just months after the Old Trafford crowd had demanded his head.

Robins, who enjoyed a colourful career as a striker, knew a potential hitman when he saw one – and in Lolley he saw great potential and was grateful to John Morris for helping bring him to Huddersfield. When the deal was concluded, Robins could not hide his delight – or his hopes for the boy who could have ended up a forgotten name in non-league. Robins said, 'There's been a lot of speculation about this deal in recent days and so we're delighted to add Joe to our squad at last. He's a promising talent and was highly sought-after, so it's testament to the club that he's chosen to come to Huddersfield Town. Joe can play off the right side of the attack or through the centre, as he possesses good pace and ability on the ball, but most importantly he has an eye for goal, as his extraordinary goalscoring record in the lower echelons of English football shows. We will be working with Joe as he adapts to the rigours of Championship football and that will take a little time, but we believe we have a very exciting player on our hands. It is really important that while Joe can get better and better, he has the ability to make an impact immediately. Joe's acquisition fits perfectly with the club's clear ethos of bringing in talented, young, hungry players with lots of long-term development in them.'

The second non-league hopeful Vardy's agent brought to the ranks of professional football was Jamie Insall. The forward moved from Stourbridge in the tenth tier to Hibernian in Scotland in September 2015, on a three-year deal. Insall, twenty-two, was thrilled to be given his big chance and told Scotland's *Daily Record* newspaper, 'This is a great move for me – I'm absolutely delighted to have been given the chance to sign for Hibs. My aim now is to repay the faith that the manager has shown in me working hard, developing my game and ultimately helping the first team by scoring goals.

'It's a big step up, but I've waited a long time for my opportunity step up to full time football and I'm determined to make the most of it by doing everything I can to succeed.'

Insall said he believed that his progress from the non-league would stand him in good stead – that it was a strong grounding from which to develop. He said, 'Playing in non-league football down South has given me a good grounding and, although I'm still quite raw, I've got a real hunger to kick on and make the most of my chance here at Hibs.'

Hibs boss Alan Stubbs was also convinced the player could make the grade in pro footie and that he would now develop still further with top-class guidance – just as Vardy believes his academy graduates will benefit at V9. Stubbs said, 'We're pleased to have Jamie signed up for the next few years. Jamie has impressed on trial and he's earned his chance at taking the step up to professional football. We feel he's got the potential to succeed at the club and he now has the opportunity to work hard and develop his game with us.'

Stourbridge boss Gary Hackett was also pleased that one of his players had been given the chance to prove he could make it in the professional game. He said, 'Hibs came in for him out of the blue, really, and everything went from there. We can't fault the way they've gone about it. Obviously Jamie was not on a contract so they had no obligation to us, but they've been very understanding and professional, and they've made a small payment to us as a token of goodwill, which is very much appreciated. It goes without saying that everybody at the club is delighted for Jamie, and we wish him well. It's a tremendous opportunity for him.'

Lolley and Insall were examples of how the V9 Academy might produce similar gems from non-league. With Vardy's enthusiasm and John Morris's talent to set up deals it would surely unearth some stars, wouldn't it? Vardy's academy plan had already earned nods of approval from many Football League officials, who believed it would be beneficial in easing the link from non-league, and Vardy is looking forward to its opening in 2017 and to playing his part in its development and, hopefully, the development of players like himself. As a way of giving something back to the arena that had helped him go on to achieve his own dreams, it was a great idea and something that

Jamie was able to support wholeheartedly, given his enthusiasm and desire to see others follow in his own footsteps.

Vardy would provide the backing and encouragement, while Morris would provide the contacts book and deals to get the stars of the academy into the Football League. It is a blueprint that will surely succeed and could well be followed by others in the years to come. If English football can promote from within, rather than bringing budget players in from the Continent, it will help the development of the game in the home of football and will also be a fillip for the England national team if more homegrown talents like Vardy can emerge.

Of course, not all who stepped up from non-league would survive when taken on in the Football League. Ben Frempah, for example, signed for Leicester themselves with great hopes in 2013. He was a big strong centre-back and was immediately compared to ex-England great Sol Campbell with similar hopes entertained for his future. One Foxes fan purred, 'Next Rio Ferdinand, can see us getting £30 million for him one day.' Another said, 'What a tank!' while another commented, 'Played forty-five minutes against Southampton's U21s on Monday. Age eighteen, plays centre-half. Similar to Chris Smalling, aerial defender. Former club is Welling United.'

And the EVO football consultancy, a consultation service providing support and expertise in the development of footballers, coaches and clubs from junior level through to professional, also welcomed his big opportunity at Leicester. They said in a statement, 'Ben Frempah has earned himself a professional contract at Leicester City, Ben has made the move jumping seven league levels from Cray Wanderers FC. After impressing playing from the age of 17 as a key centre back at non-league level his ability was soon noticed and began to attract interest, Ben spent some time with Charlton Athletic previously but was not offered a contract.

'Ben also went on trial with league two leaders Chesterfield who showed strong interest to sign him for the 1st team, however in the meantime the opportunity for Ben to trial with Leicester came about and Ben grabbed it with both hands and after just a couple of days he was offered a professional contract. Ben is very highly rated throughout non-league and has been tipped already to follow a similar path as Chris Smalling. These stories are inspiring for young players and show that by working hard in the lower leagues at a young age [you] can really get recognition. Ben is delighted to have achieved his dream. He stated this is what he has been working so hard for years and it's hard to sink in but he is now looking forward to the new challenges ahead.'

But Ben was then released from Leicester and headed north to Scottish Premiership outfit Ross County in July 2014. That also did not work out and he left the club in May 2015. Not that Ben was the only one to go: boss Jim McIntyre released thirteen others, too! The club had just escaped the lottery of the play-offs that could have seen them relegated and McIntyre told BBC Scotland, 'It's been a huge squad effort to turn around our season. Everyone has played a part. It goes without saying I wish all the boys every success in their future careers.'

Ben made just eight appearances for the Scottish outfit and

was back playing in non-league in the 2015 season, turning out for Isthmian League club Hendon. A talented player, his future was not certain as this book went to the printers. Ben's experiences showed just how tough the challenge is for non-league players to get into the Football League – and how it is just as tough to stay there.

After Vardy, you would probably say that Leicester's next most influential non-league star was another top-notch striker: Kevin Phillips. Sure, he did not come to the King Power from non-league – but he certainly started out there plying his trade and trying to make the big time. Kevin joined the Foxes in 2014 and played his part in the club's promotion gallop in the Championship. But he started out in much more humble surroundings thirteen years earlier, beginning his career at non-league Baldock Town. He spent three years as a semi-pro at Baldock but, like Vardy and many others, had suffered initial disappointment when he was younger and trying to make the grade at a league club. Whereas Vardy was released by Sheffield Wednesday, Phillips, who was born in Hitchin, Hertfordshire, suffered agony at Southampton. It was particularly upsetting, as he had been at the club since the age of twelve, spending six years of his life there. He started out on schoolboy terms and was taken on as an apprentice in 1989.

Even then, Kevin had dreams of making it as a centre-forward but was told he was too small to play up front and instead had to find a slot at right-back, and even made two appearances for the reserves in that position in 1990. He was doing his best to knuckle down so that when D-Day came – and he was either kept on or let go – he would hopefully be retained. Even though he did not want to be a full-back, he did not complain – although he made it clear he did still harbour hopes of being given a proper chance to show his worth upfront.

Unfortunately, his manager at the time did not see it that way. It does seem to be a common thread in almost all the cases I have researched that kids rejected from pro clubs are deemed too small, not having the right aptitude or attitude, or are simply not deemed good enough. Yet in many cases they still do make the breakthrough – and they have not grown much taller or filled out much muscle-wise, or changed their personality or determination to succeed. So maybe it is that they just aren't fancied by a particular manager at a particular time, that it is indeed down to fate in that, if the 'wrong' manager is at a club when they are due to graduate, they ain't gonna be taken on.

If the manager at the time warms to a player, then the chances are they will get a more receptive outcome.

In Kevin's case, the man who would make the decision on his future was then Saints boss Chris Nicholl, a former muscular, no-nonsense centre-back who had plied his trade as a player at Southampton from 1977 to 1983. He had returned to manage the club in 1985 and stayed in the hot seat until 1991.

But when the fateful day that the five-foot, eight-inch apprentice, Kevin Phillips, arrived at his door to learn if he had a future with the club, Nicholl told him he was 'out the door', saying he was too small to be a top-class striker and that his body was not muscular enough for professional football. Phillips would say later, 'I was at Southampton for six years, four as a schoolboy and two as an apprentice. I was a right-back but was released because of my physique, as my body hadn't grown fully. It was heartbreaking because all I ever wanted to do was be a professional footballer. I always remember my last words to Chris Nicholl when I walked out of his office were, "I'll prove you wrong."'

He had failed to make the grade at Southampton and had now been released by Nicholl. Ironically, Kevin would join the Saints twelve years later and grab twenty-two goals in sixty-four appearances for the club that had rejected him. But, back in 1991, Kevin returned to Hertfordshire, understandably low but determined to prove Nicholl wrong, but also – and more importantly for his own self-esteem – to prove to himself that he could cut it as a goalscorer. Even now, fate would play a key role in his development. He started off as a defender upon joining non-league Hitchin Town but quickly moved upfront – and Kevin would never again move back . . . or look back. An injury crisis led to boss Ian Allinson asking Kevin if he fancied a go upfront – and Kevin did not need asking twice.

Kevin immediately hit the goal trail, scoring twice in his first game in his new role. Like Jamie Vardy, he might not have been an Emile Heskey-style bull of a centre-forward, but he was fast, hard to stop and regularly hit the back of the net. Like Vardy, Phillips had that belief in himself – and a fierce determination to succeed and prove those doubters wrong, the ones who had said he wasn't big enough or good enough to be a professional striker.

Phillips would later be the first to admit he owed a debt to

Baldock boss Allinson for throwing him in at the deep end – and having trust in him. It would have been easy for Allinson to drop him from the attack when the club's injury crisis eased but he kept faith in him. Allinson was a striker/winger himself in his playing days, making eighty-three appearances for Arsenal and scoring sixteen goals for the Gunners from 1983 to 1987. So he knew a thing or two about what makes a good forward. Indeed, under George Graham's management at Highbury he even managed to keep the mercurial Charlie Nicholas out of the team, and in his best spell at the club scored eight goals in eleven games.

The Arsenal official club website remembers his time with them with fondness, emphasising just how talented a forward he was. A talent that led him to see similar ability in non-league Kevin Phillips when he enabled him to begin his transformation from nondescript journeyman full-back to England international centre-forward – a similar journey to that later embarked upon by Vardy.

Arsenal.com said of Allinson, 'New manager George Graham got the most out of Allinson. A record of 30 appearances as a substitute represents just over a third of his total Arsenal career – as much as anyone in the one- or two-sub era. Undoubtedly, Allinson's greatest night came at White Hart Lane in the Littlewoods Cup Semi-Final of 1987 . . . on 82 minutes he brought Arsenal level . . . [he] spun a shot through the legs of Richard Gough to beat Ray Clemence at the near post. Then, in injury time, his driven shot deflected to David Rocastle, who swept his way into Arsenal folklore with a dramatic winner.'

Kevin Phillips would never forget what Hitchin Town and Allinson did for him – just as Vardy would also make a point of saying how much his non-league experiences had stood him in good stead and helped to mould the player and man he would become. In 2008 Phillips told a press conference, 'I was a centre-forward but Southampton gave it the old "you weren't big enough, you're a late developer, get yourself at right-back for two years". If they had decided to sign me as a professional at right-back then I probably wouldn't be where I am now because my route ahead would have been in that position. I owe a lot to my old manager at non-League Ian Allinson who gave me a game up front at Baldock and I never looked back after that.

'I wouldn't have been as successful as a right-back, no chance, I might have made a career, I don't know, but I always wanted to be a centre-forward. I played all my games as an apprentice at right-back, then I got released went into non-League and then you're jumping from kids' football to men's football. Trying to play right-back when you're only a five-foot-six-or-seven-inch apprentice against men was difficult. So I didn't play too many games at right-back in non-league but then we were struggling for a centre-forward one game and I put my hand up and said I'd have a go because that is what I always wanted to do.

'I played my first game, scored two goals and never looked back. It was a lucky opportunity that came through injury. We needed someone up there, so I volunteered.'

There was no stopping the boy now. It was inevitable that league clubs would come sniffing around as news of his goalscoring ability spread – again, just like Vardy. He caught the eye of Watford, signing for the club in 1994 for £10,000 plus four subsequent £5,000 increments. He made fifty-four appearances for the club, scoring twenty-three goals – almost a one-in-two return. It was no surprise that bigger clubs coveted his talents and he left Vicarage Road in a £325,000 deal in June 1997, moving to Sunderland, where he would now grab 115 goals in 209 league games.

There was more to come, much more. Just as Vardy went on that record-breaking consecutive-goalscoring run in the 2015–16 season, so Phillips would now become the Premier League's top scorer in the 1999–2000 campaign. And, just as Jamie's run beat the previous record of Ruud van Nistelrooy and earned him acclaim right across Europe, so Kevin's top-scorer achievements as the new millennium dawned made him a household name across the Continent, too.

The reason why was simple: that remarkable goal tally earned him the European Golden Shoe award. To this day, he remains the only Englishman to win the trophy – although maybe Vardy will have something to say about that as he too knocks down goalscoring landmarks. In October 2014, Phillips told Sky Sports how much winning the Golden Shoe back then still meant to him, as he considered the relative values of Luis Suarez, Lionel Messi and Cristiano Ronaldo, who had also won the honour. Phillips said, 'Luis Suarez picked up the Golden Shoe award he's sharing with Cristiano Ronaldo this week and it brought back memories of when I won the same trophy when I was at Sunderland. It seems an age ago but it was a major honour and one of the highlights of my career. Certainly nowadays, getting twenty in the Premier League is a major, major thing, so to get thirty league goals in the Premier League in 1999–2000 was special – but I certainly didn't have any idea I was even in the running for the European Golden Shoe. I didn't even know it existed until the season finished!

'It wasn't until people reeled off the names I was competing with that it really sunk in what an achievement it was. It was fantastic to win it, though, and when I look at the likes of Ronaldo and Lionel Messi picking it up for little old me to be sat in between that lot, I'm very proud of that.'

By the time Phillips arrived at Leicester in 2014 he had certainly had some career for a boy rejected by the professional club he had been with for years as a youngster, and who had then learned to love the game again in the non-league arena. No doubt he and Jamie would have had conversations about how they had both been in that position once upon a time when they met up at the King Power in 2014. Jamie had arrived at the club in the summer of 2012 and Kevin in January 2014 on a short-term contract that would take him to the summer of that year.

It was announced he would wear the number 28 shirt and he was eager to get started in what would be his final club in a fine career. Then City manager Nigel Pearson was delighted to have snapped up the forty-year-old, as he felt Phillips could weigh in on the final leg of the Foxes' promotion push. With his wealth of experience and eye for a goal – 246 in 580 games – Phillips could prove to be a great asset. Pearson said, 'The opportunity to sign a player of Kevin's experience and know-how doesn't come along too often, so I'm delighted that we've been able to add him to our squad. He's a player I know well. He's a fantastic professional with multiple promotions to his name and he will bring some great qualities to the group, both on and off the pitch.'

Kevin was a free agent after leaving Crystal Palace, who had also benefited from his presence – he helped them win promotion to the Premier League the previous season by scoring their winning, extra-time penalty in the Championship Play-Off Final at Wembley.

It was a clever move by Pearson, because Phillips now did exactly what the boss wanted. Kevin ensured the players stayed cool and calm as they edged ever closer to the Promised Land of the Premier League and chipped in with a couple of goals in the twelve appearances he made. Ironically, given the nature of this book, Kevin would make his debut for the Foxes mid-January against Leeds United, coming on as a second-half substitute for . . . Jamie Vardy!

As one player was moving towards Leicester legend in his career, another was winding down his own incredible career, at the same club. The baton from non-league to the record books was being passed on by one ace striker to another. From European goal-scoring king to the Premier League's own record breaker with those brilliant consecutive goal strikes.

Leicester would end the season as Championship winners with 102 points from their forty-six games, nine points ahead of runners-up Burnley. In February, Kevin headed home his first goal for the club in the 1–0 win over Bournemouth at Dean Court. It was Leicester's ninth league win in a row. There had been some controversy over whether the ball had actually fully crossed the line, but boss Pearson was more interested in praising Phillips, telling the press, 'Kevin Phillips is a striker and is smiling. He knows he's scored. I have not had a clear look at the incident and the goal but the assistant seemed pretty sure it went over the line. I know that he will contribute very positively to our season both in terms of what he can do on the pitch and off the field as well. He has a lot of experience.

'He's a goalscorer and his anticipation is excellent. He's in his forties, so won't be as quick as he was sixteen years ago, but still creates a lot of space and time for himself because of his understanding of the game.'

Phillips scored his first goal at home for the club – and his second overall – in the 3–1 victory over another of his old clubs, Blackpool, a month later. Again coming on as a sub, he fired home three minutes from time, converting a pass from midfielder Kevin Drinkwater. After the game, Phillips was asked if he fancied another season back in the Premier League if the Foxes were, as expected, promoted. He told reporters, 'Do I fancy another crack at the Premier League? To be honest, I don't really want to be answering that question just yet. Who knows? I just want to get over the finishing line as I'll have some difficult decisions to make in the summer. I had a crack at it this year and I'd like to think I could still do a job. But I just want to get another promotion with Leicester and then we'll see what happens.

'We keep rolling on, we'll keep steaming on and getting as many points as we can. It's a very strong position. We have a run of fixtures coming up but if we keep playing well we can beat anyone. It's not difficult to keep our feet on the ground. In fact it's even more so as we want to keep the unbeaten run going. There are goals we want to achieve. Can we get the highest number of points of all and keep the unbeaten run going? If we break records along the way that's great. But we want to get promoted as quickly as possible. When you get promoted you want to be champions.'

Maybe he was playing shy over another stab at the Prem as he had already decided he would retire at the end of the current campaign – although he would not reveal that decision until a month later. Kevin announced the end of his career as a player on 28 April 2014. The final game of the season – Leicester's home match with Doncaster – would be his own final game. But, as a bonus, he revealed that he would stay with the club in a coaching role. That was good news for Jamie Vardy, as Phillips would now be able to guide him and pass on his own invaluable experience.

Kevin told BBC Sport, 'It is the right time to bow out. The body has been aching in the morning for a while now, especially the cold mornings with my ankles. Have I got another pre-season in me? Yes, I probably have, but I'm going to take a rest and look forward to the future.' He had set another record – by becoming Leicester's oldest ever outfield player and scorer.

He told reporters that he had also been pleased to join 'an exclusive group of three other players who have played in the Premier League as forty-year-olds' – which he did with Crystal

Palace. He anticipated that bowing out at home in front of the Leicester fans who had so taken to him would be special. Kevin said, 'All my family will be at the King Power Stadium this weekend and it's going to be emotional. However, although it's going to be a strange feeling leaving the pitch for the final time as a player, now's the right time.'

Footie fans throughout the game were united in their good wishes for his retirement. One said, 'Smashing player, lovely bloke. I hope he remains involved with the game in some shape or form. Good luck to you, Kevin, and enjoy your retirement!' Another piped up with, 'An absolute legend and a nice man too, very humble despite his achievements. His partnership with Niall Quinn when they were at Sunderland was incredible. Great professional and a class act.' And another added, 'One of my all-time favourite players, and he never played for the club I support. Fantastic.'

The actual result in Phillips's last match was Leicester 1 Doncaster 0, with fellow striker David Nugent scoring the winner. But the biggest cheer of the afternoon came when Kevin was subbed on sixty-five minutes, heralding the end of his twenty-year career. Afterwards, an emotional Phillips told the press he had enjoyed his big day and that he now planned to help Leicester boss Nigel Pearson inspire the Foxes in the Premier League the following season. Kevin said, 'It was nice to finish with a win. It would've been nice to have got a goal. The ovation was incredible. When you go to bed you kind of think of things like that. For me it was a special day and that was a special reception I got. I thought I'd be very emotional but

I wasn't. I just tried to enjoy it. I was just praying for that one opportunity I could get but it didn't come my way.

'We got the penalty, though, and that allowed us to win the game and end the season on a high, which is what we wanted. I thank the gaffer for starting me and then bringing me off at the right time. I look forward to the coming weeks and months and the next adventure in my life. There's an opportunity to come on board in a coaching capacity and I want to take my media work to a new level, so for me it is exciting times. I won't be one of those ex-pros with nothing to do except play golf.'

Kevin loved his spell as a coach at the King Power and stayed in the role under new boss Claudio Ranieri until September 2015. He then decided to move on and found a role as new Derby boss Paul Clements's assistant. Clements admitted he was 'chuffed' to have secured Kevin's services and paid tribute to Leicester for ameliorating the move, telling Derby's website, 'I'm delighted that Kevin Phillips is joining my coaching staff. He will complement the excellent individuals and skills that we have on the coaching team already. Kevin enjoyed an illustrious playing career. He was successful at a number of clubs, experienced being promoted to the Premier League on several occasions and his goal-scoring record certainly demonstrates what an excellent striker he was. He is now embracing a new pathway in his career and has successfully made the transition from player to coach in the last year at Leicester. I believe Kevin has a lot to offer with his skills and expertise and I would like to thank Leicester for their cooperation in allowing Kevin to join us.'

And all at Leicester wished the player all the best and thanked him for his efforts and services, with the club website summing up the general feeling that he had done a good job, saying, 'Phillips has recently been passing on his experience to Leicester City's attackers in his capacity as First Team Coach and Striker Mentor. He has also contributed to the Foxes' cause on the pitch. After being signed by Nigel Pearson in January 2014, he set up David Nugent for a winner against Leeds United on his debut before becoming the Club's oldest-ever goalscorer in a 1–0 win over AFC Bournemouth. It was a game that gave City a record ninth consecutive league win en route to their 2013/14 Championship title victory – Phillips's fifth promotion as a player.

'Phillips's influence and coaching expertise continued to prove vital on the Club's return to the Premier League. This past summer, Kevin was central to the coaching setup that aided a successful managerial transition, ensuring the squad's preparation for the 2015/16 campaign was successfully managed through the early stages of pre-season. Everyone at the Club would like to thank Kevin for his fine contribution as a Leicester City coach and player over three seasons and wish him the very best in the future.'

It was a generous and fair tribute from the Foxes. Phillips had played his part on and off the pitch and had made his mark while working with Jamie Vardy. Two months later, Vardy was called into the England squad and Phillips made his views clear on the man he had played with as a co-striker and also coached at Leicester. He told *The Sun*, 'In the season when I scored 30 I started a couple of games for England and because I didn't score two or three goals in the games I started, people just said you're not good enough. It's brutal when you play for your country. People are waiting to knock you. But what Jamie will do if he plays down the middle is create opportunities.

'I'd love to see him get off the mark in the next two games and play down the middle. I know Roy [Hodgson] has said in the press that Jamie should just be happy and play in the England squad and play wherever he is chosen which is fine and Jamie will do.

'But in my experience at Leicester, if you want the best out of Jamie you have to play him down the middle. We toyed with him out wide left and we didn't get what we wanted out of Jamie. He'll run up and down, he'll chase, but Jamie is a striker and likes to play on the shoulder and get in behind people and stretch teams. This is the perfect opportunity to start him in one of these two games and have a toy around. You could play him with Wayne Rooney or Harry Kane in behind him.'

Phillips also outlined why Jamie deserved his chance and how he had improved and developed as a striker even in the twenty months Kevin had been at Leicester. He added, 'I've got to hold my hands up and say he's surprised me this season. His biggest improvement has been his composure. Jamie's finishing last year summed up what he's about as a person – he's very lively and gives 100 per cent in everything he does.

'When you're in front of goal you need to be a bit more composed. Some of his finishes this year have shown me that he's certainly taken on board not just what I've told him but what other coaches have told him. It really hit home when he scored his two against Arsenal this season when he slotted both in the bottom corner. Last year he would have gone for power and pace and probably would have missed them. He's got something very unique which is unbelievable pace and if you couple that with a cool head in front of goal then you have one hell of a player.'

And he was convinced that Vardy could be England's hero if he was given a starting role at Euro 2016, saying, 'Jamie is playing in an era where you have Harry Kane, Wayne Rooney, Daniel Sturridge and Danny Welbeck when they're fit but after that, can you really name any others who are pressing? There is no real out-and-out striker that has something that Jamie has.

'He has a wonderful opportunity now if he continues to do what he's doing at club level he could really cement his place in that England squad for a long, long time. And if he goes to the Euros in the summer I would love to see him get on the pitch – unlike I did at Euro 2000!'

You couldn't really ask for a more reasoned, measured and ultimately reliable reference. Like Vardy, Phillips had grafted after initial rejection at a league club, working in non-league and then making the most of his chance when the pro clubs came calling. Like Vardy, he had proved wrong those who said he was not big enough to be a centre-forward. And, like Vardy, he had scored the goals that answered all the doubts and put the doubters firmly in their place. He had even ended up coaching Jamie at Leicester.

If anyone could assess Vardy's talent and his place in the

pantheon of current British strikers, it was Phillips. And, as *The Guardian* pointed out, Vardy had improved precisely because he had worked with Phillips at Leicester, saying, 'Leicester's staff point to the way Vardy has worked on refining his finishing skills by recognising the importance of placement over power at times – his brilliant opening goal against Arsenal this season was a case in point – and in doing so acknowledge the part that Kevin Phillips, the club's former first-team coach, played in that process.' From non-league entities to international stars: that's Jamie Vardy and Kevin Phillips.

And there are notable others who have trudged the same path as Vardy and ended their careers covered in glory, as we shall touch upon in the next chapter.

CHAPTER SIXTEEN

DIAMONDS IN THE ROUGH

Of course, Vardy and Phillips weren't the first talented players to move from non-league to the Football League. Nor were the famed Leicester City duo the only ones to make it to the top flight of English football from the depths of the amateur game. Indeed, it is possible to make a line-up of players who made the top of the game after following a similar path to the one Jamie took. A team of players from goalkeeper to striker, an eleven-man outfit plus substitutes. Vardy's academy project is designed to speed up the moves from non-league to pro football, but players of quality have emerged over the years, albeit more sporadically and less frequently.

If you were thinking of a top keeper, for example, how about the best in England for starters? Yes, England No. 1 Joe Hart signed for Manchester City from Shrewsbury Town after making his debut for the Shrews while they were in the Conference. With more than one hundred Premier League clean sheets, Joe holds the record for the most Prem Golden Glove award with four and has fifty-seven international caps since his debut in 2008. He has won the Premier League twice with City and won a great accolade in 2015, when one of the world's best keepers for the last decade hailed him as the best in the world. Italy's No. 1, Gianluigi Buffon, told reporters, 'I've been watching his game for a few years now, and Joe Hart is now for me one of the top three goalkeepers in the world. He had the period where he made some mistakes and was dropped, but he needed that. I've always said you need to be a bit of a masochist to be a top goalkeeper and that period would have made Joe that. Since his return to the team after being dropped, you won't think of a better goalkeeper in the world. It's not just about the saves he makes, but the way he organises with such confidence. He is a real leader.'

Joe joined City on 24 May 2006. He was nineteen and had made fifty-four appearances for the Shrews. He agreed a four-year deal and then City chief executive Alistair Mackintosh said, 'Joe's signing reflects the club's commitment to attracting the best young English players.' It was reported at the time that City had paid an initial fee of £600,000, which could rise to £1.5 million. But, in 2012, former City chairman John Wardle revealed that the club had got Joe for a much more competitive price after then boss Stuart Pearce and then goalkeeping coach Tim Flowers badgered him to bring Hart to the club.

Wardle told the *Manchester Evening News*, 'Originally

Shrewsbury were after £400,000 for Joe. Tim and Stuart came to see me in my office and told me he was a fantastic prospect and that we should buy him. I told them we didn't have any money, but I found some. I remember Tim said to me he's going to be an absolute star, a future England goalkeeper and how right he has proved to be. We did some bartering with Shrewsbury and got him for £100,000. I'm not saying this to blow my own trumpet. It's not me who deserves any credit, it's them who put forward their views so strongly to me – and they proved to be absolutely right. Stuart Pearce wanted him and Tim Flowers was right in his assessment of Joe.'

It doesn't end there. If you were looking for a top-class backline in front of Joe, you could do a lot worse than look at Chris Smalling, Ashley Williams, Craig Dawson and Neil Taylor. Smalling is now a fixture in England's central defence and could stay there for the next decade with likely partner John Stones. Big Chris has come a hell of a long way from his non-league days and, like Vardy, is one of the best examples of how you can aim for the very top even when you seem stuck in non-league. Like many other non-leaguers, Chris started out at a pro club's academy – in his case Millwall – but then left and headed into non-league, joining Maidstone United.

He quit Millwall of his own accord after falling out of love with the game and spent many months away from it, instead focusing on his school work with the aim of going to university. He would say later, 'I was going to study business management at Loughborough University as I had A-levels in business studies and economics and that was the road I wanted to go down.'

Maidstone boss Alan Walker rescued him from an early exit from football, giving him his debut in the Kent Senior Cup in 2007. 'He got the hump and packed it in,' Walker told Sky Sports. 'But he came and played in our reserves. The guys were telling me he was doing well, so I went to watch him a couple of times. We stuck him in and he didn't let us down. But we'd never have dreamed that the boy would achieve what he has achieved. He was promising but he wasn't that good. It was his sheer athleticism – his height and his power – that drove him on. He was always an extremely good athlete. He could run like the wind and go all day. He was brilliant at that. But in terms of his technical ability, especially his heading, he was poor. He needed an awful lot of work on his passing as well.'

Walker felt that Smalling found his love for the game once again because of his non-league exertions – that playing non-league was good for him. So when Fulham came in for him he was re-energised and had the taste for the game, with a desire to move up and move on. Walker believes that many players benefit from non-league: he believes it gives them the hunger to better themselves, that they appreciate more what they've got, and graft all the more. That is a view Vardy can confirm and it is how he hopes his own candidates for his V9 Academy feel, too.

Jamie will be looking for their hunger, their desire and willingness to put in the long hours and improve. Those assets, plus natural ability, will mean the V9 could be a stepping stone for non-league aces to make the Football League – and beyond, as Chris Smalling did, going from Maidstone United to Manchester United and England, and possibly to be a future captain of both. 'Knowing lots of non-league players, I think what happens is that the lads who've come through that route have been at the bottom of the pile,' Walker added. 'They appreciate what they've got.'

Chris said that playing non-league had made him mentally and physically stronger. He was certainly willing to learn and progress. And it was under the much-criticised Louis van Gaal that he truly progressed from a defender with potential into the player United skipper Wayne Rooney claimed was 'one of the five best defenders in the world'. Jamie Vardy has said himself that commitment and graft on the training field polished up his own game and helped him become a feared striker in the Premier League. And Smalling backs that opinion – it is the hard hours he spent with Van Gaal at United's Carrington training complex that brought about his own quite remarkable transformation.

From being a defender some labelled lightweight and prone to all-too-regular mistakes, Chris became an overnight sensation. Only, of course, it wasn't overnight: it was the result of hour after hour of learning to cut out the mistakes and being a tank of a centre-half, whom strikers now knew they would have a real battle against. At the end of May 2015, Van Gaal gave the ultimate seal of approval to Smalling's evolution by naming him Man United skipper for the clash with Arsenal. And the Dutchman said, 'I have watched and observed Chris Smalling. I shall name a captain as a human being, not only a player who passes from A to B but how you deal with your players. I believe he has been a leader of our defence.'

A month earlier Van Gaal had rewarded him for his fine form by awarding him a new contract that would run until 2019. Van Gaal again emphasised how impressed he had been with Smalling's development, telling www.manutd.com, 'Chris has improved and developed immensely during the short time that I have been at the club and has become an integral part of the first-team squad. He always conducts himself in a very professional manner and it is also pleasing that he has scored some important goals this season too. I am delighted he has signed a new contract.'

And Smalling himself told of his own delight at the way things had panned out, saying, 'I'm delighted to sign my new contract. I am so proud to play for such a great club. We have developed as a team over the course of the season under Louis van Gaal and we are now playing as a complete unit. This is a very exciting time to be at Manchester United, we are all determined to get back to where we belong and competing at the highest level.'

They could have been the form of words Jamie Vardy used at the King Power Stadium after his record-breaking scoring run in 2015. Like Smalling, he had made it to the very top of the British game from the realms of non-league. They had both worked hard to achieve their dream – and neither was complacent or satisfied with where he was at now. The hunger to achieve even more spurred them both on – and it was their non-league experiences that had played a big part in their development. Both knew what it was like being on the bottom rungs of the ladder and that gratitude for what they now had was inspirational as they strove to achieve even greater heights in their careers.

Chris admitted as much when he spoke to the press before he came up against Vardy and Leicester at the end of November 2015. He told how his non-league experiences had made him more grounded, saying, 'It's one job getting here but it's ten times harder making sure you stay here. There's so much competition and this club is always seeking the best players, so I think you've got that drive to make sure that you deserve your place in the team. If you do have a bad game, then you can look back and see how far you have come. For example, we didn't have changing rooms in non-league football like the ones we see nowadays. Sometimes I'd be better off getting changed in my car!'

Chris also applauded Vardy for his brilliant breakthrough, describing the Foxes striker as a 'hidden gem'. He said, 'With Jamie's success, I think you will see clubs having a little bit more of a look in non-league for players. If you can find some sort of hidden gems in local or non-league football, I think it would be a no-brainer to give them a chance. Jamie is such a laid-back character. Everyone's talking about him and he's doing great things this season, but you can tell he's the kind of lad that is not going to change. He takes everything in his stride.'

Chris has become rated as one of England's top centre-halves but can also play at right-back, much as Branislav Ivanović does at Chelsea. The Serb is also a natural centre-back but has excelled at full-back; ditto Smalling. If you were trying to pin down arguably the best full-back for the other flank from non-league to the pro game, Stuart Pearce would take some beating. The rugged, no-nonsense left-back started out as a trainee electrician while playing part-time for Wealdstone when Coventry signed him in 1983. He played for the Sky Blues for two years before making the move that would make him as a player and a man. In 1985 the genius who was Brian Clough snapped him up and turned him into a world-class left-back for Nottingham Forest and England. And Clough's influence would even extend beyond Pearce's playing days as he stepped up yet another level to become a manager of some repute. He would go on to manage Manchester City, Nottingham Forest, the Great Britain Olympic team and even be England's caretaker boss.

Yet it all began at Wealdstone in the Alliance Premier League, where he was first choice full-back for five years. And even when he arrived at Forest he was still unsure of whether he would make the grade, or even like pro football, and put an ad in the club's matchday programme advertising his services as an electrician! He needn't have worried. Such was his talent, commitment and ferocious will to win that Clough made him club captain – a role he carried out with distinction for twelve years.

In 2000, Pearce told *The Guardian* how his non-league days had spurred him on to enjoy his full-time career as a pro – and to make it last as long as he possibly could. He said, 'It wasn't until after a couple of years at Forest that I realised I probably was good enough. I didn't know whether it was going to work for me or not, but I did have a qualification as an electrician.

The fact that I was a late starter and missed my first five years may have been a spur to play on longer.'

From non-league to footballing Hall of Fame – that would be Pearce's destiny, as he is now one of the great names honoured at the National Football Museum, where he is described thus: 'Stuart Pearce is one of England's greatest defenders; a tough-tackling, no-nonsense full-back with a terrific left foot which helped him register 87 career goals. A Nottingham Forest legend, Pearce will always be remembered for two penalties; his saved effort at Italia '90 and subsequent redemption during Euro '96. Working as an electrician, Pearce spent five years in non-league with Wealdstone, before signing a first professional contract with Coventry City in 1983. After more than 50 games for the Sky Blues, Pearce made the move to Nottingham Forest, joining Brian Clough for what proved to be one of the most successful periods in the club's history. During 12 years at Forest, Pearce amassed 401 appearances, many of them as captain, scoring 63 goals. Pearce won two League Cups with Forest and was an FA Cup runner up, scoring the first goal in the 1991 final (though the match was eventually lost 2–1 to Tottenham).

'Pearce also spent 12 years as an England international, making 78 appearances. Reaching the semi-finals of the World Cup in 1990 and European Championships in 1996, Pearce suffered double disappointment as England lost both matches to the Germans on penalties. Pearce was the third oldest outfield player to appear for England; a testament to his career longevity.'

Not at all bad for a guy who started off at the bottom in

non-league! Stories like Pearce's are what made Jamie Vardy confident there was room for him, too, at the top table. And they are what helped inspire him to set up his own academy. Having been at the coalface of the non-league arena, Jamie knows how to dig his way out – and how to help other 'hidden gems' do the same. The guys who are chosen for his annual V9 sessions will be lucky guys indeed, as they will be encouraged by Vardy, who has been there, got the T-shirt and found the exit door to stardom, riches and global recognition as one of the great centre-forwards of the modern era.

Pearce is also convinced that non-league can provide more stars in the future. In November 2013, he presented a cheque for £50,000 to Basford United as part of Budweiser's Club Futures programme. And he explained how non-league was a force for the good. He said, 'I was lucky that, when I was at school, the caretaker played himself. He took five of us into the local non-league team. Without that, I'm not sure what direction my football career would have taken. Clubs like this, clubs that give opportunities to young players, are vital when it comes to keeping young people fit and to give them the chance to be part of a team environment. It gives them something to focus on.'

It was also telling in June 2015, when Liverpool signed Danny Ings from Burnley and some pundits questioned whether he was good enough or had the right to play for such a world-famous club, given that he had only one year's experience in the Premier League. Pearce was the first to step up and defend Ings's right to a top-flight opportunity, branding his critics as 'snobby'. Pearce told 888sport, 'We all have different career paths. I came through from the non-league system so if you're going to be snobby about it I'd have never kicked a ball in the top flight. The bottom line is he's obviously a big talent and a decent player to add to the squad.'

At the peak of Pearce's career, he would come up against a striker who also had to struggle – like Jamie Vardy – to break through from non-league to the Football League. Yes, that man was Arsenal legend and now TV pundit Ian Wright. An extraordinary goalscorer for the Gunners, Wrighty would admit that the desire to prove he was good enough and, like Pearce and Vardy, to make up for lost time as he too was a late bloomer inspired him to be better than the rest when he got his big chance. He would later admit that it was football or nothing, as, unlike Pearce, he had no skills in other fields. He could not have been an electrician or a chippie. He would say, 'I was a useless labourer, I was a useless bricklayer, I was a useless plasterer.'

In his autobiography, *The Wright Stuff*, he also explained his inspiration to reach the top, saying, 'I draw my strength and desire from the fact I came into the game late. You want to show people, prove that you are good enough. All the people who rejected me when I was younger must look at it and know they were wrong.'

He may have been useless as a plasterer but that is what he feared he might end up as, after his unsuccessful trials with Brighton and Southend in his late teens. He looked set for a job as a plasterer who played non-league football. But, while playing for non-league Greenwich Borough, he was spotted by a scout for Crystal Palace and invited for a trial. He impressed Palace manager Steve Coppell, who had starred as a winger for Man United and England and knew a bit about strikers. Wright signed professional terms for Crystal Palace in August 1985, just three months short of his twenty-second birthday. Like those of Jamie Vardy, his goalscoring exploits would become the stuff of legend. Wright spent six years at Palace and seven at Arsenal. At Highbury, he helped the club win the Premier League, the FA Cup, the League Cup and the European Cup Winners' Cup. Ian played over 500 games in England and Scotland, scoring almost a goal every two games. He also won thirty-three caps for England, weighing in with nine goals.

Arsenal FC are sure of his position in their club history – he will be for ever a goalscoring legend. The club described him in these terms in their list of 'Gunners' 50 Greatest Players': 'Some footballers are great goalscorers. Others are scorers of great goals. Ian Wright was both. The Arsenal legend always found a way to find the net, whether it required a sumptuous 30-yard chip or a toe-poke from two yards. Wright's repertoire of goals made him one of the finest – and most explosive – strikers to grace the English game. And, of course, he was a showman. Wright was a force of nature on and off the pitch, assuming the mantle of practical joker in the dressing room and choreographing a string of theatrical goal celebrations. No wonder Arsenal fans loved "Ian Wright Wright Wright". The man himself was late on the scene in football terms – he signed professional terms for Crystal Palace in August 1985, just three months short of his twenty-second birthday. It seems strange now but, when he moved to Arsenal in September 1991 for a club record £2.5 million, some questioned the wisdom of the transfer.'

By the time he had hit a record number of goals, no one – club officials or fans – was questioning either his worth or his legacy. The man who had come from non-league as a late starter – just like Vardy – would always have a place in their hearts. Ian was rated No. 4 in that all-time Gunners Top 50, behind only Tony Adams, Dennis Bergkamp and No. 1 Thierry Henry. Like Lineker, Wright would eventually carve out a career in broadcasting, as a TV football pundit.

Ian is a regular presenter on Absolute Radio and they gave him this gushing résumé for a glittering career – from non-league to TV and radio star, saying, 'Ian Wright needs virtually no introduction. As a footballer, Ian played for Crystal Palace, Arsenal, West Ham, Nottingham Forest, Celtic, Burnley and England. During his celebrated career with Arsenal he lifted the Premier League title, both major domestic trophies, and the European Cup Winners' Cup as well as becoming the club's leading scorer.

'When he finally retired from the game at the end of the 2000 season, he became a TV presenter with shows including his own late-night chat show *Friday Night's All Wright*, *Gladiators* and *Friends Like These*. Wrighty's long and illustrious career means he's a well-respected pundit and he spent the 2014 World Cup as part of the ITV commentary team. He's also a long-standing columnist for *The Sun* newspaper. In 2000 he was awarded an MBE in tribute to his sporting career.'

Funnily enough, Stuart Pearce has also made a name for himself as a radio pundit, on TalkSPORT, and is also an MBE, while Gary Lineker is arguably the king of football broadcasting – and an OBE. So maybe the road for Jamie Vardy could also yet have twists and turns on radio and TV – and even an honour for services to football and England at Buck House! Certainly, Pearce, Smalling and Wright have shown that there can be honour-strewn pro careers for those who make the step up from non-league. It is no pipe dream that you can be playing non-league – and a year later be in the England squad, as Jamie has proved.

Another former non-leaguer who has made the big-time in the modern era and could yet be a dark horse for the England squad is former QPR striker Charlie Austin.

And, as with Vardy and many others, the story takes a similar start with the player being rejected as a youth, this time at Reading. Also like many, Austin was told he was too small, not big enough to have a future in the league. After being shown the door by Reading in 2005, he now took the path also taken by Vardy as he headed into non-league football. In another nod to Vardy, Austin also worked part-time as a tradesman to support his football dream. Austin would lay bricks, all the while daydreaming about the time when he would be taken on as a pro and earn his living that way. It may have been a daydream but, as with Jamie Vardy, it was backed up by a burning desire to prove wrong the people who had said he was not good enough – and to prove to himself that not only was he good enough to play in the Football League, he was good enough to play at the top: in the Premier League and even for the England national team.

Austin would stay in non-league from 2006 to 2009, playing for four teams. He started off at Kintbury Rangers, moving on to Hungerford Town, Thatcham Town and Poole Town, before finally arriving at Swindon in 2009. In 2014, Austin told *The Independent* how life was before he made it to Swindon, explaining how his semi-pro wages at Poole supplemented what he earned working for his dad's brickworks firm. He said, 'I earned decent money on the yard but it was difficult work, from 7.30 in the morning to 4.30 in the afternoon. It's not nice getting up at 6am, when it's pitch black and you have to get in a van with 10 other lads, to go and work in a muddy building site in the winter, and not get home until 5.30 or 6. That was the reality of it.'

His forty-six goals in forty-six games for Poole Town, which helped them win the title, changed his life dramatically as the Football League clubs started to circle. Swindon boss Danny Wilson was the man who eventually put his money where his mouth was and he made his Football League debut in the league match away at Norwich on 24 October 2009, coming on as a second-half sub. Almost a month later, he scored his first professional goal in the third minute of his full debut away at Carlisle.

After thirty-one goals in fifty-four appearances for Swindon, it was time to move upwards again. Austin headed North to Burnley for a two-year stay and kept up his goalscoring feats with a one-in-two ratio of forty-one in eighty-two games. He made the record books at Turf Moor by becoming only the second-ever Burnley player to score twenty goals before the end of November, matching club legend Andy Lochhead's feat of 1966.

Soon it was time for another move and, like Vardy again, Austin packed his bags and headed South. In August 2013, he signed for Queens Park Rangers in a deal that would make him financially secure. Burnley accepted that they simply could not compete with the terms on offer at Loftus Road and reluctantly accepted they had lost the player – although grateful for the goals he had scored. The club issued a press statement, saying, 'The Clarets striker has signed a three-year-deal at Loftus Road, bringing to an end his two-and-a-half year stay at Turf Moor. CEO Lee Hoos said, "We worked very hard to keep Charlie at Burnley and we are sorry to see him go. However, we were unable to compete with the package on offer from Queens Park Rangers, a club in receipt of the largest parachute payments in history and able to offer what are effectively Premier League wages in the Championship. Charlie has been the subject of a lot of attention from a lot of clubs, but has handled himself in an extremely professional manner in his dealings with us, in what has been a difficult time for both him and the club.

'"While we very disappointed and sorry to see him go, this will create an opportunity for another player. Our priority now is to focus on making a strong start to the season. Longer term, we will continue to build the club in a prudent and responsible manner in compliance with Financial Fair Play Rules."

'In closing, Burnley Football Club would like to thank Charlie for his contribution in the past two-and-a-half years and wish him well in his future career.'

But Rangers boss Harry Redknapp was delighted to have got his man. For a fee reported to be in the region of £4 million, he had hit the jackpot. Austin brought a guarantee of goals and Redknapp knew that could be the difference between promotion to the Premier League and another season in the Championship. He said, 'Charlie's an out-and-out goalscorer and we're delighted to have him here. He's scored goals wherever he's played throughout his career and I'm very confident he'll take his game to the next level with us. I've got no doubt that if we give him the right service he will score a lot of goals for us. He's young, he's hungry and he's up for the challenge of helping us get out of this division.'

Austin also believed this was the right move as he charted his seemingly inexorable rise to the very top. He said, 'I'm really pleased to be here. Harry spoke to me at length about the ambition of the club and the desire to return to the Premier League and that's where I want to be as well with QPR.

'This is a really exciting time for me and I can't wait to pull on the QPR shirt for the first time. I'll come in, give my all and hopefully score the goals that ensure we have a memorable season.'

By 1 January 2016, Austin had scored forty-five goals in eighty-two games for the club, thus maintaining his one-in-two games ratio. It was enough to get them promoted to the top flight but not enough to keep them there. On 21 May 2015,

Austin's career line, which had followed a similar path from non-league as Vardy's, dovetailed perfectly. This was when the two of them were called up for the first time for England duty for a friendly match against Ireland and a Euro 2016 qualifier against Slovenia. Austin did not feature in the match, but it showed just how far he had come. And the Vardy comparisons are remarkable, almost a mirror image.

And in January 2016 Charlie rejoined Jamie in the Premier League when Southampton sneaked in to snap him up for an absolutely bargain fee of £4 million.

Other strikers have also shown the same grit and determination to make it from non-league like Vardy. Grant Holt of Wigan started out at Workington while also working as a tyre fitter. And West Brom's Rickie Lambert joined local club Liverpool at ten, was released at fifteen and turned out for little Marine and worked at a beetroot factory before his career got back on track, and he eventually ended up at Southampton.

Running the gamut of rejection, playing non-league, being transferred to a professional league club, hitting the big time, and even becoming an England international – it is truly remarkable how Jamie Vardy's fairy-tale rise to the top applies to other footballers in England. Tapping the non-league market is surely the way to go for more top clubs now that they can see for sure the results such a policy can yield. Vardy's story is the best known and, as such, he may have given others the belief that they too can now expect to tread a similar path if they put in the hard graft and have natural talent.

Yes, Jamie Vardy's legacy may well be more than the goals

record he earned at Leicester or his impact on the Premier League – he may well go down in history as the trailblazer who opened the floodgates for countless other non-league footballers who dared to dream after observing his fairy-tale rise from the very bottom to the very top.

CHAPTER SEVENTEEN

JAMIE VARDY'S 'AVIN' A PARTY

By February 2016, Jamie Vardy was indeed ''avin' a party'. A remarkable 3–1 win at Manchester City on the sixth of the month put him and his teammates six points clear at the top of the Premier League. They had played twenty-five games with just thirteen to go, and by now even the most sceptical of pundits were beginning to shrug their shoulders when it was suggested the Foxes could win the league, and answering, 'Maybe.' 'No chance' had now turned to 'maybe' as the 5,000-to-1 outsiders from the start of the season refused to surrender their spot at the top. It had been the defeat of title favourites Man City at the Etihad that had most confounded the doubters in a campaign straight from the realms of fairy tales.

But, even after this victory, boss Ranieri refused to go overboard, still insisting his team were only outside contenders for the title. He told BBC Sport, 'We played very, very compact and believed everything could be possible. We play without pressure because we don't have to win the league. We must enjoy. This league is so strange and now it is important to think about Arsenal. I want to wait until the end of April because I know the last matches are very tough. This is a fantastic moment for the Premier League. Nobody knows who can win it.'

Jamie also insisted it was premature to indulge in such conversations, although he, like his teammates, enjoyed playing with the freedom that the lack of pressure, because they were outsiders, allowed. He played as if he was enjoying a kickabout with pals in the park and was clearly enjoying his football. He even had time for a spot of fun with the Man City fans who barracked him when he missed a chance in the second half. He turned round with a smile on his face and reminded them of the score at that particular time by holding up three fingers on his right hand and making a zero with his left!

The great thing here was that while some fans replied with jeers, most had a smile on their faces and enjoyed the banter. They knew that this boy had achieved so much from nothing, and admired him for that and the fact he was the top scorer in the Premier League just four years after playing in non-league. He may have helped punish their own team but he had also shown what a great player – and a great sport – he was.

Jamie had failed to find the net in Manchester that early Saturday kick-off but had scored arguably the Goal of the Season in the previous match against Liverpool at the King Power. He latched on to a superb pass from Mahrez thirty yards out and struck the ball home on the volley, giving hapless Kop keeper Simon Mignolet no chance. The wonder shot was timed as flying at 64 m.p.h., and Vardy himself said it was the best he had ever scored. He told *The Sun*, 'I don't think I will ever score a better one to be fair. But a goal is a goal and more importantly it's three points. I watched their keeper and he was coming quite far off his line. As soon as the ball came through and bounced, I just took my chance and luckily it went over him.'

That was typical of the humility Jamie feels when describing his own feats of brilliance. But Ranieri and Liverpool boss Jürgen Klopp were rather more lavish in their praise of one of the greatest goals ever witnessed in the Premier League. Ranieri said, 'It was a fantastic goal – an unbelievable pass from Riyad Mahrez and unbelievable what Vardy did.' Kopp added, 'It was a world-class goal. It's nice to be in the stadium when he scores – but in an ideal world you are not the manager of the other team! We had the ball in their box and didn't shoot – one second later Vardy scored. That says everything about the game.'

There were obvious comparisons between Jamie's goal and that scored by Dutch legend Marco van Basten in the 1988 European Championships. Russia were the fall guys back then, as the Holland genius scored with a fantastic long-range volley after a great cross by teammate Arnold Mühren. Ranieri compared the Vardy goal to that one and added that it also reminded him of a sweet strike by Roma striker Francesco Totti in Italy's Serie A. Ranieri said, 'I can put him with Van Basten, when he makes a fantastic goal. And I don't know if you watched Totti when he scored against Sampdoria. Amazing goals. I don't know if it's a new talent this season. Jamie, what he is doing is fantastic. Good for him, good for us. Good for our fans. You can only clap. What else can you do?'

Fans on social-media sites also talked up the 'English Van Basten', with many arguing that there was now no way England boss Roy Hodgson could ignore his claims for a starting place, if fit, for Euro 2016 in France. One fan summed up the general feeling, saying, 'You don't have to watch Vardy play for too long to realise that he is that true rarity, a born goalscorer. When he scored that fantastic goal on Tuesday [against Liverpool] you could see him immediately size up the situation before striking the ball. And his second [the same night] was pure goal poacher/lethal finisher. His success this season is no flash in the pan.'

Leicester legend Gary Lineker also chipped in, saying the goal was 'the goal of the decade', while Dutch hero Ruud Gullit added it was 'a fantastic goal'.

There is no doubting that Jamie Vardy had come of age; that wonder striker was the icing on the cake of a season in which he had not simply come to prominence but had gatecrashed the door marked 'Future Leicester legend'. It also remained to be seen if he could achieve the same sort of distinction at England level. He had proved he could score goals – and plenty of them – in the English top flight; now the whole country waited with bated breath to see if he could repeat the goals rush with England at Euro 2016 and beyond.

That goal against Liverpool had been a real moment to treasure as it added to Jamie's growing worldwide reputation, but a goal four days earlier also meant a lot to him. Jamie was on target as Leicester beat Stoke 3–0 at the King Power on Saturday, 23 January 2016. It was another typical Vardy goal as he took control of the ball, raced goalwards and rounded the keeper to slot the ball home in the sixty-sixth minute. It made the score 2–0 and helped to start the Foxes on the road to a comprehensive win that put them three points clear at the top of the table. But, from a personal point of view, it left Jamie feeling relieved, as it was his first goal in eight games. It ended a drought that had seen him without a goal in the league for more than ten hours, and silenced the critics, who had started to write him off after his record-breaking run of goals.

It proved that he was no flash-in-the-pan and that he was a team player. Throughout his seven-game barren run Jamie had played for the team and helped others to get on the scoresheet. He had known all along that he would return to goalscoring form and never worried that he had lost his touch. *The Sun* summed up his goal, pointing out, 'Jamie Vardy has bottle as well as brilliance . . . holding his nerve to net a trademark goal and end a barren seven-match run.'

And Ranieri said he had never worried about Jamie not scoring for a few games and that he had told him not to worry, telling the Associated Press, 'Jamie I tell every day it is not important [the drought], although I know goals for the strikers is important and maybe now he has more confidence. When I speak with him I say it is important you continue to work hard because you are the main man and if you start to press then everyone follows. Then sooner or later you score a goal, I tell him this. You have to work and make it happen and then the goal will arrive.'

Even *The Sunday Times* acknowledged Jamie's brilliance and position of growing prestige by naming him among its '500 most influential people in Britain in 2016'. It introduced the section with the following statement of explanation: 'Who is shaping our national life in 2016? This list of the 500 most influential people in Britain today, compiled by Debrett's, presents a fascinating kaleidoscope of the individuals who have a real impact on every aspect of our lives. Influence takes many forms, from the political power to make laws and command national budgets, to the creativity and charisma to get you tuning in to your favourite television shows – or YouTube channels. What all the people on this list, from sectors including finance, the arts, politics, sport, food and technology, have in common is that through a combination of talent, originality, hard work, persistence, courage and, occasionally, good luck they have earned the right to make a difference.'

And of Jamie himself, they commented in the subsection on sporting heroes of the era, 'Jamie Vardy, footballer, scored in eleven consecutive matches as his team, Leicester City, topped the Premier League after battling to avoid relegation last season.' It was an indication yet again of just how far he had come – from nowhere to a place in the most influential list in one of Britain's 'poshest' newspapers. Quite a step up from working in a factory in four years.

And sister paper *The Times* also got in on the act, asking Matt Reeves, the strength-and-conditioning coach at Leicester, to reveal some of the secrets behind Jamie's astonishing rise. Reeves said Jamie had only 6 per cent body fat, which even by sporting standards was exceptional, and that this helped him with his speed and performance on match days. He also revealed Jamie was not one of those players who spend hours in the gym, restricted already by the blue cast he wears on his wrist, but that the player knew naturally how to use his 'strength and aggression effectively'. Because he is such an explosive player, Vardy needs longer to recover after matches, with Reeves telling how he is carefully monitored after games. The fitness coach also revealed how the player makes good use of a facility many footballers would probably shy away from. Reeves admitted Jamie makes 'the most of Leicester City's new cryochamber unit, in which players are exposed to temperatures of minus 135°C!'

It was all good for Jamie as he moved towards the run-in for the season in the middle of February 2016. He was on a high and so were Leicester, and he would improve the feel-good factor around the King Power Stadium by signing a new deal that would tie him to Leicester City FC until the summer of 2019. He had signed new terms that would keep him at the club for a further year beyond his existing deal. In a statement, he outlined his joy at the new deal, saying, 'I'm absolutely delighted to be fighting to achieve something special with this club, as part of this squad. I've never known a spirit like it – from the owners, to the manager and his staff, the players and the fans. I want to be part of it for a long time. Leicester City have shown nothing but total faith in me since the day I arrived here three-and-a-half years ago and it's impossible to measure how much that belief has helped me to improve. I'll forever be grateful for the investment the Club has made in me and I'll spend every day working to repay it.'

City boss Ranieri added, 'Jamie is a fighter. He has had an unbelievable journey to get to this point in his career and continues to play every game as if it's his last. I love his spirit, which is a quality I want in my players above all else. He has shown what a fantastic player he is and, more importantly, he is part of a fantastic group. I am very happy that he will stay with us for a long time.'

It was claimed in the press that Vardy would net around £80,000 a week, a significant increase on his current £45,000-a-week deal. A cliché maybe, but it wasn't just about the money for Jamie – he did feel a bond and affinity with the club. Both player and club were fighters against the odds; in that sense they were made for each other. They were ideal companions as they battled together along the road to unexpected glory in 2016 – the boy from nowhere and his team from nowhere.

CHAPTER EIGHTEEN

CRÈME DE LA PREM

It would be somewhat ironic that the games which meant Leicester had finally won the league would be ones in which Jamie Vardy did not contribute. Or, more precisely, had no part to play on the pitch. He was certainly vociferous on the sidelines, urging his team-mates on frantically, along with others who were not in the playing squad at Old Trafford on Sunday 1 May, 2016 – and cheering Chelsea to a remarkable comeback against Tottenham the following night.

Mayday indeed on the Sunday, but in Leicester's case it was hardly a distress call; more a call to arms as the team put in one final massive shift to earn a deserved 1–1 draw at Manchester United. Then they all congregated at Jamie's home the next night - and celebrated madly as Chelsea fought back from 2–0 down to draw 2–2 with Spurs and send the championship trophy to the King Power Stadium for the first time.

Leicester City Football Club – champions of England. A sentence surely no one never expected to hear in our lifetimes. No one could have anticipated it at the start of a 2015-16 season in which most pundits and fans expected them to finish mid-table, at best. Or, at worst, claw their way to safety in another untidy relegation scrap. Indeed, they were 5,000-1 rank outsiders to lift the title with the bookies – and it's not very often that those money-men call it so wonderfully wrong.

But, no, the Foxes were Premier League champions – and deservedly so. They had led the table for the majority of the season and consistently proved they were worthy of all the garlands and accolades that now inevitably came their way. They had the PFA Player of the Year in Riyad Mahrez, the Manager of the Season in Claudio Ranieri and the prolific marksman whose glut of goals had underpinned their claim for greatness – and who pushed team-mate Mahrez so close for that Player award – in Jamie Vardy.

Vardy, who would lift the Football Writers' Player of the Year gong just before the United match, had proved that he could not only bridge the gap between non-league and Premier League, but that he could also be rightly justified in claiming he was now a talent worthy of being showcased on the highest of stages - with England in Euro 2016 and probably the World Cup of 2018, and in the Champions League, club football's ultimate competition, with Leicester.

And before we all start up coming over all pessimistic again, and say they will never even get past the group stage, let's not forget the precedent set by another Midlands club 30-odd years earlier who everyone also predicted would be out at the first hurdle. Yes, let's contemplate the remarkable Nottingham

Forest of that era, who won the then European Cup for two consecutive seasons after coming from nowhere to win the English league, like Leicester, under the inimitable genius that was Brian Clough.

And as Forest had Trevor Francis, so Leicester have the brilliant Vardy. And as Francis had the wizardry of John Robertson on the wing, so Vardy is blessed with the similarly unstoppable talents of Mahrez.

It is an uncanny similarity, so let's certainly not write off Leicester in the Champions League too swiftly, as we did in the Premier League this time around.

That Mayday draw at United was the icing on the cake for the team and Vardy, but also frustrating for their master marksmen. As we have often pointed out in this biography, you have to take both sides of the man when you place your trust in him as your talisman. Vardy the goal poacher, but also Vardy the firebrand. Like many fine strikers, it is the fire in his belly that helps create the goal machine.

But occasionally that fire brims over and there is a price to pay. Jamie Vardy pays lip service to no one: he is his own man and sometimes oversteps the mark, as we have noted in previous chapters. For the majority of the campaign, he managed to keep his emotions – and that quickfire temper – under wraps. But if presented with a scenario that he believes is genuinely unjust, he can lose it – and Leicester can lose him.

Such a scenario presented itself when he was sent off by ref Jon Moss in City's 2-2 draw against West Ham on 17 April. He was sent off for diving in the second half, an indiscretion that earned him a second yellow card, and he shouted angrily at Moss as he left the field. It meant he missed the next match, at home to Swansea, for a one-match ban but also had to sit out the game at Old Trafford too as the FA imposed an extra one-game suspension for abusing Moss. It was a cruel twist for a man who had done more than most to take the Foxes to the summit, but they then showed they are far from being a one-man outfit as they crushed Swansea 4-0, and then tied with United to secure the crucial point that would ultimately clinch them the crown.

Of course, Jamie had done more than his bit for the team during the run-in, with his two goals at Sunderland on 10 April meaning they beat the Wearsiders 2-0 and were now bang on target to win the title barring any late collapse of form. Sure, it was his first goal in open play since February, but it had hardly been a case of his form deteriorating or him hiding away because he had lost his goal touch. During that six-game barren goals spell he had still contributed massively to the team as they ground out wins *a la* the Arsenal sides of old (with five 1-0 triumphs). And he did score in consecutive games for England during that period, so it wasn't as if his goal touch had deserted him completely.

As Jamie has often said, the team's performance and result is the most important aspect of the affair – and in that respect he did not let them down as they marched unrelentingly onwards and upwards towards that groundbreaking first top-flight title. The pressure continued to build around the club as they moved ever closer and it wasn't helped as the statisticians now regularly trotted out the fact that they had never won the old First Division, let alone the Premier League, in their existence as a professional football club since 1884. The history books beckoned, but so did the increased stresses of trying to make it into them and not to falter at the final hurdle.

Those two goals by Vardy at the Stadium of Light meant he had equalled Gary Lineker's 20-goal haul in the 1984–85 season. Lineker tweeted that it was a brilliant achievement and Jamie admitted he was delighted to have matched Gary's goals output. After the game he said, 'It is massive for me personally. Coming off, the Sunderland fans were clapping us as well which is brilliant. It was a great game, we knew it would be tough but we managed to grind it out. It's a step close to possibly winning the league. We'll enjoy the rest of the day and then get back to training for the next week.'

His boss was just as pleased with his brace of goals. Ranieri said, 'It was important for Jamie to score. He made some good assists in our last game but he is our goalscorer and he needed to score again. I am very happy with him.'

The victory meant the Foxes were now just three wins away from lifting that elusive top-flight crown and that they were guaranteed Champions League football. They were seven points clear of second-placed Tottenham, with five games to go. For some, the achievement of making the Champions League would have been enough – but not for Vardy and his team-mates and their charmingly idiosyncratic manager. They wanted it all, and they wanted it now. There would be that slight stumble in the following match, as they drew 2-2 at home to West Ham, and Vardy saw red, but they would prove emphatically once again that they were made of stern stuff.

When the crown was finally won, there could be no doubting they were worthy winners and that they were, without doubt, the best football team in the country in terms of dedication, determination, confidence, team spirit – and no little talent, too. Those attributes applied also individually to

Jamie Vardy. The boy from nowhere had proved he belonged right here in the big time. His goals had powered the boys from the King Power to a rightful first Premier League crown and he had prospered on the big stage, laughing in the faces of those who had dismissed him as not good enough: those who claimed he was a lower league talent punching above his weight in the top division.

Jamie Vardy had proved all the doubters wrong as he proudly paraded his Premier League winner's medal. This was a footballer who had arrived late in the big time – but who was now making up for lost time. He had won the league, he was set to be a part of a successful England team as Euro 2016 loomed ever closer and faced the prospect of testing himself against the likes of Messi, Neymar and Ronaldo in the Champions League in the 2016-17 season. Knowing Jamie, he would do all that, and not look out of place.

From non-league to the Premier League, the Champions League and an England shirt. Yes, such a rise against all the odds is certainly a story worthy of Hollywood if ever I saw one.